Peter Anderson Graham

Nature in Books

Some Studies in Biography

Peter Anderson Graham

Nature in Books
Some Studies in Biography

ISBN/EAN: 9783337028541

Printed in Europe, USA, Canada, Australia, Japan

Cover: Foto ©Thomas Meinert / pixelio.de

More available books at **www.hansebooks.com**

NATURE IN BOOKS

SOME STUDIES IN BIOGRAPHY

BY

P. ANDERSON GRAHAM

LONDON
Methuen and Co.
18 BURY STREET, W.C.
1891

TO

THE MEMORY OF

MY MOTHER

I DEDICATE

THIS LITTLE VOLUME.

CONTENTS

INTRODUCTION

WHEN youth's fiery ardour begins to show the first symptoms of decay, and the mind, like the joints, is losing its suppleness, the hue of Pleasure seems to undergo a corresponding change. In early days the bright-eyed, frank, and easy damsel had a rosy colour that suited her merry face. She hardly asked to be wooed, but of her own accord was a guest, not only

'—— when to the trembling string
The dance gaed through the lighted ha','

but all the day and every day. Nay, at times of blackest melancholy, when the young heart was whelmed in hopeless despair, did she not from some unseen corner launch her soft mockery? What would we not give for that glimpse of her shining eyes, caught when, 'sighing like a furnace,' we bade her a solemn farewell; for during the heyday of youth she was a close and dear companion, who came alike to labour and to play, and whom not disappointment, nor sorrow nor hardship, nor defeat, could permanently banish.

A few years pass by and lo, the erstwhile girlish figure has aged more swiftly than her lover, and grown into a grave and sober Pleasure, and one who, as

capricious as ever, chooses only a rare and occasional
hour for her quiet visit.   If we are very instant
in search of her, she hides a face that, though more
sombre than of yore, still is pure and unsoiled, and
sends us a false shape of Pleasure that is no more than
a cunning disguisal of Care, her enemy.   And after
pretending to romp and play with us in the old way, lo,
the traitress pulls off her mask, and the momentary enchantment is broken.   There is an empty purse, a head-
ache, a deranged liver, and the clinging embrace of
Care.

He, I think, who woos Pleasure in field and coppice
and walks with her on purple moorland, where blue
sky is the only roof, is slowest to discover any falling
off in the beneficent sweetness of his mistress.   With
others, the ruling passion that began by yielding delight ends in becoming a tyrant.   The devotee of
wealth or fame, even after accomplishing his desire, is
still a bondman.   For renown does not come till the
heart is withered in its search, and the dear circle of
those who would have shared it, is narrowing to an
end; while, long ere riches have been accumulated, the
joys to be bought with them pall upon a jaded mind.
But while our senses endure, they will not cease to be
gratified with the music and pageantry of earth.   When
the ear has grown weary, not only of human intercourse, but of old tunes, and instruments, and songs,
it still will listen with content, while the summer wind,
travelling over field and sea, sighs out the faint low

melody it has sung to past generations—the melody it croons above their graves, and plays to their children. Till the dim tired eyes have closed out the light forever, Spring's green that fades into summer brown, and after flashing out in a transient gleam of gold and purple, dies in white, will be the most beautiful and refreshing of things seen.

And the chief excellence of this delight is that it is accorded, not only to those who have cultivated it during years of solitude and contemplation, but to the greater number who, engaged in the world's endless strife and arduous pursuits, see but a casual and occasional interlude of rest in Nature. Yet their comfort is derived less from actual Pleasure, than from Pleasure's faint sweet sister. For the fragrant goddess, whose shrine is among the tall ferns, and under the oak-boughs, answers like an echo to the tones of her lover. If he carry a weary and disappointed heart to her for solace, the blowing wind will sing to him of buried hopes, and the running water shall murmur a tale of sadness.

It is only those who are happy themselves who can detect any gladness in the wild bird's carol, or be merry within hearing of the sea's monotonous lament. Nevertheless, amid all this lamentation of things about to perish, there grows up a feeling of content that is almost happiness, mirthless and subdued, but pure and perfect.

The pleasure that resides in art is identical with that which dwells in Nature. What the writer or

painter does is to catch and fix for all time the vision
or emotion, or impression that yielded pain or pleasure
to him. In a seeming paradox, it may be said that he
singles out and stays the pregnant moments; for the
only material he can work upon is his own experience.
The life he has lived, the beauty he has seen, the joy,
pain, love, loss, regret, hope, triumph, sorrow, he has
felt; the dreams and fancies that have come to him—
these are what he may set forth in his chosen medium.
And the selection of form is really of consequence to
himself alone; the only supreme necessity being for
him to take that over which he has most complete
mastery. The story told to Bevis by the brook in
Wood Magic is not less pleasing because it is as rhyme-
less as the water's voice. And yet it may be granted
that verse is the finer instrument of expression; its
very lilt and harmony helping words to signify more
than is in any dictionary. In an 'idle dream,' such as
has come to many a poet, as he rested or sauntered by
familiar streams, faint winds of thought and fancy blow
across the mind, nourishing ideas that the most consummate art is hardly able to convey with any fulness
or adequacy; but it is something if the music of the
lines, the sound of the words, the ring and rhythm of
the syllables create in the imagination of the reader an
atmosphere akin to that of the writer. Prose is incapable of similar modulation, though there are passages in Thoreau, Jefferies, and Carlyle,—to take
examples of men apparently incapable of writing their

best in rhyme—that linger in the mind as tenaciously as any poetry.

Out of the books he has read every free and intelligent reader makes a private anthology of his own, and is probably at times dismayed to think what a thin little volume it would be if materialised in print and binding. Do you not. pick and choose even among Shakespeare's plays, and the stories of Scott, and the prose of Addison ? Nay, in the very briefest of your favourite works—in *Hamlet*, or the *Lotos Eaters*, or *Lycidas*—are more than a very few lines really part of you—bone of your bone, flesh of your flesh ? The rest may be both read and admired, but is practically forgotten. It does not work itself into your language, and become the expression of your thought ; it does not get itself set to a tune, and at times unconsciously hummed as one will catch one's-self humming ' Fear no more the heat of the sun,' or Herrick's ' Daffodils,' or ' Had we never loved sae blindly,' or ' Queen and huntress chaste and fair,' or 'The King sits in Dunfermline toun, drinking the blude-red wine.' Not the great majority of books only, but the greater portion of every book, far from being admitted into the inner sanctuary of thought, excites but a transitory gleam of pain or pleasure then drifts into the great stream of things moving to oblivion.

It is the same with existence itself. If we look back, how few seem the unforgettable moments of full, bounding, thrilling, pulsating life ; how numerous the blank spaces whereon Time's noiseless feet have left

neither print nor record. Of the train of hours ceaselessly streaming past us, each bearing its little burden
of pain, or joy, or passion, how few has memory rescued
from the thronging current eternally rushing to forgetfulness! Here and there one because it winged its way
so swiftly, here and there one because it crept so pain-
fully on leaden foot! But be they sad or merry, these
hours (eternal because unforgotten) are, as Mr. Henley
sings the poems of life,

> 'Lived but left unsung,
> The best of all.'

A vast library of books is read, and the mind is enriched with only a very few lines; a generation is lived
through, and a little handful of memories is all that is
left of the experience.

It is strange how few impressions produced, even
by Mother Earth herself, pass into and become an ineffaceable portion of one's existence. Will appears to
have no say in the transaction. We travel hither and
thither in search of the picturesque and fancy we can
say with William Wordsworth

> 'The sounding cataract
> Haunted me like a passion : the tall rock,
> The mountain and the deep and gloomy wood,
> Their colours and their forms, were then to me
> An appetite.'

But lo, the unguided hand of memory, from all the rich
and beautiful sights offered for its acceptance, lays hold
of only a few of the homeliest bits of scenery, as setting
and offset to the days and hours it has gathered for

preservation. And, particularly as we grow old, I think it is to home and its landscape that the mind most frequently and most lovingly returns. It is in regard to the rill running past the door of infancy, the woody heights whereon the schoolboy birds-nested, that one again and again

> ' feels as in a pensive dream,
> When all his active powers are still,
> A distant dearness in the hill,
> A secret sweetness in the stream.'

For that reason I cannot help thinking that many critics and biographers are at fault in slurring over the period of childhood. When portions of an author's work are so much loved that they actually become part of the reader one is less anxious for information about success and failure, editions, variations and corrections, than to have some authentic image of the invisible friend with whom it is a delight to hold converse. And the picture desired is no mere physical catalogue —dealing with the height and weight of the writer, the colour of his hair and eyes, his dress and gestures; but what these are but the vesture of,—the mind and its associations. Still less advantage is there in listening to a long succession of self-appointed judges who make of literary immortality an eternal Day of Doom by leading out an author and pronouncing sentence of life or death on him. But could they show us the boy bright eyed and hopeful, unconsciously garnering treasure amid his play and frolic, and trace the growth of his mind and the accumulation of wealth that is neither to be measured by gold nor bought nor sold, they would indeed add to our pleasure.

It was my aim to attempt something of the kind in the little gallery of portraits here presented; though the subjects were chosen with the ulterior motive of illustrating the view taken of our relation to Mother Earth by some of the clearest and most contemplative minds of the century. How all that is precious in a man's work results from the union of ability with environment, of accident and endeavour, is incidentally shown by the contrasts of their history. For, indeed, it would appear that a man's success arises from his adjustment by hazard to circumstances that develop his peculiar talent. It seems at first a painful thing to contrast the struggles and hardships and suffering of men like Richard Jefferies and Robert Burns with the apparently happier beginning of a Scott or a Tennyson. And, indeed, the consideration almost makes any but a partial judgment impossible. I never think of the neglected farm-house at Coate, the ill-regulated household with its continual pinching for money, the boy's half-neglected education and his ill-directed attempts to begin a career, without loving his work still more. Yet even the misfortunes we bewail appear to have been the instruments by which his talents were developed.

So, likewise, Burns in a Lincolnshire Rectory never could have been the Burns we knew, and it is extremely doubtful if his strong and wayward genius would have flowered at all under the refined cultivation that has brought the Laureate's to perfection. Even in Carlyle, the thinker and moralist, early impressions remained all-powerful to the end. His puritan home, and border ancestry, the conventicle sermons and the frugality of Ecclefechan, are as much a part of Carlyle as the romance of Tweedside is of Scott.

Thus we must take our great men as we find them. It is entirely fatuous to reckon that it would have been better for them if this and the other thing had happened. We may in an idle hour please ourselves with dreaming what would have occurred under a re-arrangement of the decrees of fate—if Jefferies had been sent to college for example, or Lord Tennyson born in a ploughman's cottage—but the reality is absolutely hidden from us. The very circumstances against which we complain may, for aught we know, have nursed and developed in them the gifts we chiefly prize. If only we are able to see it, the life a man has lived and the words he has written are parts of the same whole. All apparent contradictions and divergences exist only because of the imperfect knowledge and insight that prevent us from seeing the harmony that does and must underlie them.

Our examples, if they do nothing else, strikingly illustrate this doctrine. Each might almost be figured as a characteristic growth of his native soil. Whoever has read *The Gamekeeper at Home, Hodge and his*

Masters, and *Wild Life in a Southern County* without knowing anything of the author, will in nowise be surprised to see him emerge from a Wiltshire farmhouse. He is as characteristic of the Downs as Lord Tennyson is of the wolds and the flats of the East Coast. From the writings of the one you could guess him to be the son of an unprosperous yeoman, from those of the other that he came from a higher grade of society. The difference in culture and refinement between the homes is reflected in the respective books. But the point at which not only they but all the others unite is in ardent love of Nature in general, and in particular of the little corner that gave them birth and formed their early impressions. The latest work of the Laureate discloses memories of Lincolnshire as vivid as the remembrance of those Wiltshire fields whose magical beauty floated round the death-bed of Jefferies.

Scott, who, in character, inclination, taste, and genius, was an incarnation of the Border spirit had even in a more pronounced degree this enduring love of home. Who, having once read, can ever forget Lockhart's account of that last and most melancholy return to Abbotsford when the sight of the Eildons, and later, of his own towers, so delighted and excited the dying man that he became almost unmanageable? And looking at his tomb in ruined Dryburgh, and listening to the eternal music of the Tweed, one is almost tempted to believe there is truth in his own words, and that, as his dust mingles with the dust he loved, 'Mute Nature

mourns her worshipper.' The more I read his novels
the more I feel assured that very often the romantic
incident was inspired by its scene: that, in other
words, the love of earth was the deepest passion of his
life.

Carlyle himself—Carlyle, who could hardly speak or
write without launching forth into the immensities and
eternities—had a rugged love all his own for the homely
Border village where he was born, and an anxiety that
his ashes should mingle with the ashes of his forefathers. And assuredly in his case the desire for
burial in the Ecclefechan churchyard arose from no
vain and idle superstition, no unworthy solicitude for
the clay garment he had worn. It was but a proof
that the last sparkle of life still turned longingly to the
scene of its birth, that in Carlyle, as well as Sir Walter,
the love of earth was a permanent passion.

In devotion, Thoreau to his native Walden, Burns to
his Ayrshire streams, Wordsworth to his northern hills,
alike evinced a passion equally intense. It was as if the
goddess of the open air inspired them with an affection
as ardent as man ever felt for woman, one that endured
to the very brink of death, one that, for all we know,
still persists on the other side of the curtain that has
rushed down between ourselves and them.

Everything born of earth is more or less subject to
the same potent witchery. The lady of our desire sings
to us in the wind and in the voice of breaking waves
and the murmur of running streams. She weeps in the

falling rain and smiles in moonlight and sunshine.
Her diadem is a jewel-work of stars and her veil is of
white cloud. In summer she clothes herself with
radiant gold and green and purple, and in winter with an
august mantle of white, edged with dusky brown where
the woods are. And whosoever shall most fittingly tell
the tale of his love for her and sing her smile, and
bewail her frown, and lament for that she is cruel, and
rejoice because she is kind—he is the true artist; for
Nature is the inspiration, art the song.

I

THE MAGIC OF THE FIELDS

(RICHARD JEFFERIES)

My first visit to Coate was paid on a merry October day. The sun shone on hedgerows ruddy with haw and tawny with withering leaf, on stubbles red with thundercups—'thin bubbles of blood'—and on banks whereto St. Martin had beguiled the gowan, the speedwell, and forget-me-not. Birds as well as flowers seemed deluded into playing at a mockery of Spring. From the oaks that Jefferies loved, from the dense and browning Wiltshire elms, cooed the lovesick ringdove; old rooks were mending their nests; the skylark poured its music from heaven, the robin from the spray; yet a vigorous autumn wind blew upon yellowing copse and spinney, scattering acorn and chestnut on the roadside, and flinging the red-cheeked apples into the grey orchard grass; an occasional horn-note from the woodlands, or the glitter of a crimson coat, told how the cub-hunters were anticipating winter; showers of loose and fluttering leaves were heralding its speedy advent. The Folly-trees were already bare, and raised their black tracery above the smooth and desolate-looking downs.

A

From the top of any hill you see the land of Jefferies all around,—uplands of grassy and broken wold, lowlands of England's most fertile soil. Here lies the raw material out of which he fashioned the glowing and beautiful country of his Essays. Be it done ever so tenderly and lovingly, it seems like an intrusion on the dead man's secret to search into the poor bare facts that his memory and imagination invested with so many moving charms. Yet if we could but look clearly into his life, and learn what preparation he underwent and what difficulties he surmounted a new light would fall on his work.

The house where he was born stands close to the roadside, separated from it only by a garden bordered by a wall and a row of limes—a comfortable, common-place-looking building. It was occupied by several generations of Jefferies, whose tombs may be seen in Chiseldon Churchyard, and traditions of whose strangeness and eccentricity still abound in the neighbourhood. Except the grandfather of Richard, a thriving but whimsical miller, whose droll figure, as he walked from Coate to Swindon, clanking behind him a chain used for fastening his trousers, is still remembered, the Jefferies appear to have been clever at everything but making and keeping money, and the tiny estate had been lost and won more than once before it finally passed out of their hands. The father of Richard was primarily installed as the miller's tenant, on whose death in 1868 it came with certain burdens into his possession. Farmer Iden in *Amaryllis* is a portrait of him, and the whole picture of the household borders sadly on fact. Too frequently one meets and loves and pities similar unfortunates. In their case the magic of the fields is a cruel and wicked witchcraft, with evil spell forcing them to toil. The observing, thoughtful, clever man, who planted his potatoes on philosophic principles, but had no taste for buying or selling or saving, was out of his element. A small farmer who would succeed must be as acute on the marketplace as a a Yorkshire tyke, as 'grippy' as a French peasant proprietor. But the elder Jefferies had no gifts in this direction, and while debt and difficulty accumulated he had only the rude resource of labouring on the soil with the energy of despair.

How the man had lost heart in the weary hopeless struggle was visible enough on the entry of his successor. Any casual passer-by might have guessed the state of affairs, for pecuniary difficulty paralyses energy as nothing else does, and the place had all the wild neglected look you find in some of the homesteads of thriftless Ireland. The thatch was full of holes, and green with sprouting wheat, so that it had to be torn off as useless and replaced with slate. No modern improvement had been introduced into the house, not even a grate to the kitchen, at whose open hearth the kettle used to be boiled over a blazing fagot. The garden had been allowed to relapse into a state of nature. Jefferies' father had a passion for hiding his house in trees, but the young saplings had never known the pruning-knife. Other evidence there was in abundance of the bitter sadness with which he left the old home, loved by the reserved and quiet man as none but himself fully knew. The common country-people in the neighbourhood never penetrated the mask under which a sensitive but kind and winning nature was concealed. But they felt he was not like themselves. He was often seen

wandering in the fields by dusk and starlight, or setting
off to Swindon at moonrise, while in the other houses
all but the goodman lingering over his last pipe had
gone to bed. Had he only known how to buy and
sell to advantage, how to raise stock and swell his
banking account, the field-lore he had collected by long
observation would have been a title to respect; in one
constantly struggling with debt and difficulties, who
dressed in any kind of coat, and who was no hand at a
bargain, his curious theories and strange ways were
contemptuously regarded as only the silly whims and
eccentricities of a good-for-nothing. Whenever the
weather failed as a topic of conversation, the peculiarities of the Jefferies formed an alternative subject for
the gossip of the country-folk. And he, feeling all
this, gave way more and more to the reserve he handed
down to his son.

Yet you feel in all the semi-autobiographical work of
Richard that his father's was the prevailing influence.
Mrs. Jefferies was never quite the same after the sad
death of her first girl, killed, while quite a baby, by a
runaway horse in front of the windows. Her successor
at the farm related a pathetic little incident to me, of
her lifting the latch of the garden gate, but refusing to
enter the old grounds, many years after she had left.
One may fancy the crowd of tender and painful, of
loving and sad, recollections associated with walls every
one of which had rung to the laughter of her children,
of spots each vivid with a vision of their playing. He
who has seen the lady of his early love the happy wife
of another may alone realise it. For the objects of home
are loved with almost a personal affection. Below the
mulberry-tree which inspired one of Richard's earliest

attempts at verse, other boys and girls run and laugh, while he who sang thus is at rest :—

> ' Oh mulberry-tree, oh mulberry-tree,
> Dear are thy spreading boughs to me ;
> Beneath their cool and friendly shade
> My earliest childhood laughed and played,
> Or, lips all stained with rich red fruit,
> Slept in the long grass at thy root.'

And now, like an untrue love, it forgetfully yields to the endearment of others. So, too, the summer-house is there, and the swing, his study window looking to the Swindon valley, the gateway leading to the pond, apple and walnut and pear tree, the very musk thrusting its leaves up between the stones—*sunt lachrymæ rerum*! If it were beyond his imagination on his deathbed to conceive 'how they manage, bird and flower, without me, to keep the calendar for them—for I noted it so carefully and lovingly, day by day,' how much more difficult to realise that the intimate and familiar treasures of generations of Jefferies are now forming the memories of alien children !

These facts help us to picture the household into which he was born. We may guess that where care was, and the shadow of advancing ruin, bitterness and irritation were also present. Nor is it credible that amid the tumbledown fortunes of the house the children were trained as lovingly and carefully as they might have been under happier circumstances. Yet there was tenderness and to spare, and when the father led his boys to look at the first skyblue eggs in the sprouting hedge, and taught them to find and name summer's wild flowers and autumn's red berries, he was doing more than is in the power of any schoolmaster. Their companions still remember the truant-playing propensities of the children, but they had no desire to escape *his* instructions. To them Richard probably owed the inborn love of reading that partially counteracted the neglect of set tasks. And the paternal influence was reinforced by that of the aunt at Sydenham with whom he was frequently sent to stay.

His true school lay around Coate, and every reader of his works is familiar with it, for the mind of no poet ever clung to the early homestead more tenaciously than his. To his dying day, and through all the horrors of his terrible illness, everything else was external to the world of his childhood. The wooded coves and margining oaks of the lake in which he and his brother launched a canoe of their own making, the hatch where at peril of their lives they sat to view the brook's barred pike and red-finned perch (now the wonder of a new generation's youthful eyes!), the hazel copses where they nutted and blackberried, all the wide fields over which they roamed, were to the last fresh and green in his memory. The idle do-nothing hours, when Richard lay in the sun, or scampered and romped with his companions, were those that were the making of him. It was then he acquired the wood-magic that enabled him to interpret the wild bird's song, and familiarised him with the weasel's cunning, and the wiles of rat and fox. He made stories for the timid and gentle hare, that, save in dead winter, when there is no other harbourage, avoided the woods as carefully as the rich traveller avoided Epping Forest in the days of Dick Turpin; what the brook sings to the rushes, what the bee hums to the flowers, were the dreams of his solitary hours. And even in manhood he retained all a child's surprised delight at the sight of a magpie's odd gestures, the flashing plumage of jays quarrelling under an oak-tree, or the autumnal parliament of rooks. In frequent times of solitude he learned to love before he had quite come to understand the cooing and warbling and chirping, the pretty quarrelling, of the birds, and the discord of shrieks that arises when thrush and blackbird and finch are alarmed by the visit of a wandering cat, or unite to repel the invasion of a predatory hawk.

Oftenest, however, as he grew up, he chose for his wandering the bare green Downs, where no one was to be met save the shepherd, and the rolling monotony is broken only by Follies or small clumps of trees. There he sat and wondered how the kestrels climbed the air, how they could hang so motionless midway between the blue and green, where they flew to when, mounting high with strong and steady wing, they fared off swift and straight into the immeasurable distance. But he had almost an equal delight in the butterflies playing on the breeze that sighed round the buxom hill or swished in the hollows. He had to an intense degree the Nature-lover's delight in the wind. Its moaning and whistling in the bare winter woods, the soft rustle of its play with the nodding corn or the foliage in harvest, its autumn lament as it plays huntsman to the chasing leaves, or bellies the elm standing like a draperied woman with her back to it, or blows tempestuously over reddening thicket and thinning hedgerow, were music and poetry to him. Among these Wiltshire Downs, too, the Romans have left many traces of their camps and trenches and ditches, and it was hardly possible that a reading and contemplative boy should play in the antique fosse and climb the mounds of it without picturing to himself the life of long ago. He was the more likely to do this, because that part of Wiltshire is not rich in those memorials of more recent strife you find so plenteously on the Borderland. From the base of the Downs it is a rich alluvial land of fat farms and neatly thatched cottages that stretches away. There is a poverty of ivied ruin and keep, such as might have filled his mind with romance and inspiration no equal to which was to be derived from the grassy mounds telling where Roman legions had fortified themselves against the tattooed Britons, although it was no unpleasant exercise to recall the uncultivated land, to repeople the deep forest with inhabitants, and to bring back the horse and foot of Cæsar.

Richard's inborn love of solitary musing was strengthened and developed by circumstances. As he grew up he began to find that he was happiest apart from companions. Like all country boys, those of the hamlet delighted in physical contest. The swiftest and strongest among them was their hero. Now, he could invent and tell a blood-curdling story, or he could even walk a long distance, and, like Wordsworth, he was an excellent skater; but in running, jumping, wrestling, and other athletic exercises, he was easily beaten. What is worse, he was of a proud, sensitive temper, and the loud laugh and rough jeer flung at the defeated, little as a boy of coarser mould would have heeded them, galled and hurt him till he braved the charge of cowardice by staying away from their mock battles. 'Their imputations,' he says in a semi-autobiographical chapter, 'stung him deeply, driving him to brood within himself.' The clouds that for ever hung over Coate lessened its attractions into conspicuous inequality with those of the meadows.

The prospect of using a gun was the opening of a new world to him. Yet I do not think he ever was a very keen or accomplished sportsman. When in later life he missed the chance of writing that book on Shooting asked from him by Mr. Charles Longman, the obstacle was probably his consciousness that he lacked experience. Mr. Besant cites the incident as illustrating his argument that 'Jefferies could never do anything which did not spring from his own brain.' But where was the lad to obtain material? I never heard that the gentlemen of Wiltshire asked him to their shooting parties, and it is doubtful if ever he fired a shot in a drive or *battue*. Nor is it likely that he, who in his most prosperous days could not muster funds to buy Sowerby's *English Wild Flowers*, could at any time have indulged a fancy for fashionable and expensive breechloaders. Besides, his writing on Sport is that of a vigilant observer, not of an enthusiastic maker of big bags. His practice was limited to the rabbits on his father's farm, with an occasional excursion to the neighbouring meadows. Nor must the *Amateur Poacher* be taken too seriously. I am told by an old companion that he and his brother used sometimes to find pocket-money by selling rabbits to old Job Brown—mentioned in *My Old Village* with a realistic touch—instead of bringing them home to the family pot, but never on any extensive scale. What he learned of true sport appears to have come mainly from a neighbouring gamekeeper, his friendship for whom accounts for more than one thing in his story.

It is a common practice for lads in his station of life, whether they are born sportsmen or not, to cultivate the acquaintance of the keeper. Of all rural occupations his is the most interesting, and every walk with him must have been to Jefferies a lesson in natural history. A keeper is always glad to have a quiet intelligent boy in his company, one with a keen eye for the bolt-holes, and a quick ear to catch the sound of a struggling rabbit in ferreting,—who likes nothing better than to look at a gin or snare, or hold a dog, carry a gun, climb a tree, or perform any other little duty incidental to his task.

In Jefferies' fine description of a burrow as an ear, or 'lug,' as King James called his contrivance for acting eavesdropper to his prisoners, you have a fancy that probably came during his wary and silent waiting by the ferreted burrow; and indeed the keeper has hardly a duty that would fail to interest the nature-loving boy. We can imagine the two walking along the headlands, or lounging through the wood, now halting to drop a jay or a magpie from its nest in the thicket, or noting to what new earth the vixen had transported her family, or resting quietly in broomy corners or sunny dykebacks, while wild things, unwitting and fearless, crept forth from their holes. And that Jefferies freely asked, and was answered, why and how one animal was killed and another allowed to escape, plainly appears from his work.

For us who look back, the life he led at this time seems almost ideally happy. So it did to himself as his childhood receded into distance. But in retrospection it is usual to forget half of the facts. Is the period remembered by one dark spot?—that spot widens like the storm-cloud, that, beginning no bigger than a man's hand, grows and darkens till all the sky is covered. Is it remembered for something sunny?—as we grow older it shows all blue and sunshine, for the clouds that were there fade away and disappear. What Jefferies in after life considered trivial and forgettable troubles were real enough while they lasted. And there is evidence and to spare that his sensitive nature winced under the trials of childhood. Not only did his figure and weakness feed the scorn of his companions, but they were exaggerated by faults and peculiarities of dress due to scarcity of money at the farm. As soon as Jefferies could afford it he clothed himself as much like other people as possible, and it is known that his nature was sensitive to the ridicule provoked by what was mistaken for the unkempt eccentricity, but was in reality the poverty, of his early years. His dislike of going to school, and, still more, his running away, proves as much. He was just sixteen when he and a companion formed a singular project of walking across Europe to Moscow, and, but that their money ran short, there never would have been any *Gamekeeper at Home*. And that adventure does not speak to his having felt much happiness at Coate.

His poaching, which perhaps accounts for the funds for this journey, was a result of shortness of cash. Every intelligent boy needs money, and Richard shrank from no legitimate means of satisfying his necessities. I say legitimate, not in defence of poaching, but because in him it was hardly an offence. When a couple of boys, instead of going to the school for which with wallet and satchel they set out, turn aside to the fields, what do they find to do there? The main idea is to catch or kill something. At first nature and accident provide an abundance of game. It is sport enough to creep softly behind an inexperienced young thrush and pass a stealthy hand over him, to hunt half-fledged

linnet or robin from bush to bush, to steal between a
young rabbit and its burrow, or chase a leveret on the
grass, and guddle trout in the stony brook. Rambles
across country produce still richer adventures. Winged
rooks and wounded pigeons after escaping the gunner
lead a skulking life in thick hedgerows and plantations; sometimes even a hawk, a jay, a magpie, or
an owl, may thus be taken. But in a while the
developing hunter longs for a weapon; and Jefferies
and his brother exhausted their ingenuity in a progress
from the primitive stick and stone to firearms. The
summer-house that still stands in the garden was their
armoury. After the period when sling and catapult no
longer satisfy the vaulting ambition of childhood, with
teacups and hazel-rods and melted lead they made themselves 'squailers'; they cut the tough brier to fashion bow
and arrow; and then they tried their first experiments
with gunpowder, delighted at first merely to produce
an explosion. In all this there was nothing beyond the
ordinary experience of a hamlet boy. But the need of
money drove Richard onward to new discoveries. Not
only were materials required for the experiments: an
equal craving of another kind had sprung up, and demanded to be satisfied. He had devoured the contents
of his father's bookcase, and now he wanted to borrow
and buy. So the result was that when he could set an
effective snare, and use a gun to purpose, he got into the
habit of selling a portion of his spoil to Job Brown.

As the novelty wore off, however, the hunter's delight
in circumvention and death grew less, and the more
refined pleasure of watching and noting increased, till
at last the only use of his gun was to lend interest to
what otherwise would have been an aimless saunter in

the fields. When once he had learned the fair and un-
fair methods of angling, when he could use the rod and
the wire with dexterity, he ceased to care for the
pursuit. You do not find that in the illness and
despair of his after life he mourned lost opportunities of
sport, or looked back with regret to happy days of
successful shooting. It was the hours of still enjoyment,
of calm, unconscious observation, that he lived again
most lovingly. He was at his best in describing the
myriad-shaped life of summer, when the implements of
death are laid aside, and not autumn, when dogs are
exploring the thicket and the brown woods are rustled
by beaters. It is important to note this, because
an entire misapprehension of his character has been
founded on the assumption that he was a Leatherstocking
of the English shires or a half-developed Nimrod. No
theory could be more fallacious. He writes neither of
dogs nor game, neither of guns nor coverts, as one who
was above all a sportsman. The part acted by sport in
his life was that in these early years it supplied him
with a new inducement to be abroad, and stimulated
him to a closer study of wild life. It also prevented
him from feeling so keenly as he might otherwise have
done the deep vexations of juvenile penury. That too
was now beginning to play its part in urging him to
activity in the battle of life.

The son of poor parents, be he ambitious or contented,
lazy or energetic, finds it necessary at an early age to
do something for his living, and the shrewd country-
folk hastened Jefferies to a decision by showing a
certain contempt for his agricultural accomplishments.
Long after his name was famous as a writer, the
be-smocked village patriarch remembers him 'nowt o' a

farmer' and 'a lazy lout on the land'; and there was
one who used to tell with pride how he had openly
rebuked the indolent loafer. To the staid bucolic mind
the lad was a puzzle and a scandal. 'When I try to
describe these things to them,' he wrote in one of his
latest essays, 'they look at me with stolid incredulity.'
In good sooth, when a young man talked to them of
'white clouds in blue summer skies,' and did not refer to
the weather, when he idled away hours in mere enjoyment of the sunshine and raved about a sparkle on the
brook, a music at the hatch, a glow and a glory of night,
the steady-going countryman shook his wise pate, and,
nodding to his neighbour, thought it a pity the youth's
upper story was going. 'See'd ye ow't on the Downs?'
one would ask as dusk was settling down on the grey
hills, and 'Nobbut Dick Jefferies moonin' about,' would
be replied. Some thought him incorrigibly lazy, and
told him so; others reckoned him half-cracked and
pitied his family. And there was that in his appearance to strengthen the latter opinion. Carefulness in
dress was not a highly prized virtue at Coate, and
Richard at that time, with his unshorn and unkempt
locks, and his untidy and badly preserved clothes hung
on a lamp-post of a body, was the picture of a sloven.
In later life he had quite conquered this bad habit of
his youth, thus making the inference a safe one that
his appearance as a boy was the result of the free-and-
easy style of living at Coate. His general aspect was
such as to exaggerate eccentricity in dress. He was
overgrown and unhealthy, tall and thin and bent, and
he shared with his brother the peculiarity of holding
his head very much to one side, and his full and bright
blue eyes peered so vacantly through the half-closed

eyelids that a familiar friend might pass him half-a-dozen times and not be seen, and at the seventh might be greeted only with a distant nod. In thought or dream or reverie, the boy was often miles away from his close companion.

There was no one to guide or help him, and so his budding and uninformed ambition soon landed him in one of the very worst places for it, viz. the office of a country newspaper. It had the solitary advantage of leading towards literature by a path whereon life could be supported during the journey. His early desire, however, was not literary fame, but the very much humbler one of earning a little money. I have been told by one of his editors that he never made himself a proficient, far less an adept, at writing shorthand; he never learned more than barely sufficed for ordinary work : a convincing proof, in a man of his strong will and tenacity, that he did not aim at making journalism more than a stepping-stone. A country reporter in a lively district such as Swindon, if he be clever at his work and enterprising, may easily earn a respectable income at a very early period of his life; for not only has he his weekly wage, but there are many little ways of augmenting it. There are news agencies that need correspondents, and local newspapers glad of paragraphs.

But success is the reward of qualities exactly the opposite of those possessed by Jefferies. The ideal reporter for a country paper is a brisk, impudent, flattering, chaffing, good humoured youth, who has not the most remote sense of personal dignity or consciousness of superiority. He starts off in the morning as trig and neat as a city clerk, drops into a favourite tobacconist's shop, and over a penny cigarette flirts with

the girl at the counter till useful customers whom he
can fish for a paragraph come in ; then he turns to a
taproom where he knows one or two local magnates
take their 'morning'; he has his associates at the
political club, the attendants at the hospital are his
friends, and he never misses an opportunity of treating
a policeman. He will make an immense fuss about
describing a tradesman's improvements, and then beg an
advertisement from him. Among the guardians and at
the Town Council meetings he has confidential friends.
There is, in a word, hardly a possibility of anything
happening without his knowledge. In the office itself
there is no end to his zeal and usefulness. He is
sub-editor and reader, paragraphist, leader-writer, anything and everything that the occasion may require.
One day he toils like a slave, on another he idles like
a loafer. Always is he greedy of an excuse to make
copy.

How was the shy, dreaming, solitude-loving boy from
the farm to fill a position such as this? The training
he had received for it was the worst possible. At Coate,
where no man was called master, independence was in
the very air, and neither Richard Jefferies nor his father
was likely to feel himself inferior before the drapers
and grocers of Swindon. Nowhere, in fact, does a feeling of mental superiority grow more swiftly than in
the country; as nowhere does stupidity more swiftly
become more stupid. It was soon a complaint made
against the young reporter that he had no proper sense
of his own position. He could neither fawn nor coax
nor flatter. Instead of asking as a favour for information, he demanded it so imperiously as to have made
legends in Swindon of his extraordinary impudence.

Nor could any sense of his own subordinate position restrain him from an unrestricted exercise of his own judgment. If sent to report the speeches of the little great men of the neighbourhood, he thought nothing of refusing to do so on what editors thought the fantastic ground that they were 'infernal rot.' In a quiet hamlet the thoughtful man never learns the chatter, the pleasant meaningless small talk, of the town. Jefferies was not fond of speaking unless he had something definite to say, and as every word of his own had a meaning, he commonly attached far more than its due importance to the idle conversation of others. And he had the additional misfortune of being constitutionally destitute of humour. Scarcely in his writing is there to be found even the feeblest glimmer of laughter, and no one remembers of his having ever made a joke. On the sort of day he esteemed most perfect—a morning of warm sunshine in spring, when the tender grass is first shooting up through its withered bed, and the scent of the budding oaks is in the lanes—his enjoyment still remained serious; he did not experience the exuberant overflow of spirit that blithens the ploughboy's whistle, and makes the shy milkmaid, she knows not why, laugh with the ploughman. He drank in beauty and enjoyment as silently as a tree or a flower. And this extreme seriousness of temperament was a drawback where flippancy and brightness are the highest virtues.

The early literary adventures of Jefferies are those of an unworldly dreamer, of a greenhorn, the smart successful townsman would say. In his position a clever lad with the mark of success on his forehead would have laid the foundation of a fortune. Undistracted by any vision of higher things, he would have reported

and paragraphed without wasting a thought on anything
above or beyond perfecting himself in his task, and
preparing for the better situation that would be his
assured reward. And the world always looks on approv-
ingly at the smug and respectable career of talented
mediocrity.

It is otherwise with the boy who has thrilled to the
magic of the fields, who has communed with nature on
the lonely hills and by the singing rivulet, and whose
musings have been lit up by the genius of every author
he could lay hands on. Hours like these nurse ideals
and ambitions, and mother strange dreams that keep
him far away from the political meetings and cases of
petty larceny and the county court broils on which the
attention of the other is concentrated. And thus in
the performance of every-day tasks the man of genius
is too frequently beaten and distanced by the commonplace matter-of-fact craftsman. Yet he feels big with
a secret ; he walks with the consciousness that one day
he will achieve something to altogether dwarf the
poor doings of his rivals. Jefferies not only had that
feeling, he was able to impress it on all with whom he
came in contact. His family felt that he had a future,
and even the provincial editors for whom he worked,
though they had cause to complain of his work, felt
that there was something in him if he could get it out.

But here lay the difficulty of the untrained lad. He
had many a bitter experience to undergo before learning
that a treasure-house of beautiful thought is unsaleable
on the marketplace until the owner has acquired the
gift of appropriate expression. And in this respect
literature is a trap to the unwary. No born genius of
a painter or a sculptor would hope to embody his con-

ceptions in artistic form until by a laborious apprenticeship he had learned to handle the chisel or brush. In
writing no such technical difficulties are apparent.
With paper, ink, and an unlimited supply of ideas, it
seems so easy to sit down and compose a masterpiece.
It was many a day before Jefferies overcame this delusion.
There was something in his mental constitution that
blinded him to it. To the end of his life his finest
thoughts and fancies centred upon the commonest
objects. It was neither by his additions to our knowledge nor the profundity of his thought that he won his
place, but by the vividness of his literary pictures.
The charm of his writing lies in its illusion. By the
spell of his imagination he gathers the Wiltshire fields
into every room where he is read.

At first, however, his capital was only this fund of
common knowledge. Underlying it was a rich but
still unmined seam of gold. What is probably the very
first of his unpublished works still exists in manuscript
in the possession of Mr. Harmer, editor of the Cirencester
paper to which, after a round of magazines, it was sent.
The title is *A True Tale of the Wiltshire Labourer*,
and the book is a realistic, almost Zolaesque, transcript
of life at Coate. Probably he chose the theme for its
simplicity, and because it lay within the range of his
knowledge. Not yet was he alive to the overwhelming difficulty of the task. I question if there is among
all the skilled novelists of our time one who could
compel a wide circle of readers to be interested in
characters so humble, in scenes so limited and sordid.
One remembers Sir Walter's saying, 'Ay, ay; if one could
but look into the heart of that little cluster of cottages,
no fear but you would find materials enow for tragedy

as well as comedy.' Human life is the same among
the Wiltshire Downs as under the shadows of Eildon,
but the attendant spirit of Jefferies was no Asmodeus,
and, so to speak, he failed to lift the thatch from any of
the cosy huts nestling lonely in dales by the rivulets
that wander through his childhood's fields. Burns and
Crabbe could make the peasant interesting on his own
account, but your modern novelist uses him only as a
foil to wealth and refinement. Jefferies began by trying
to present him with unimaginative realism, and without
poetic insight.

Human nature to the very last was a sealed book to
him. It is between laughter and tears that we watch
the immense literary activity of these years, inspired as
it was by the same sanguine hopes, the same incapacity
for practical affairs, that were exemplified in his father.
The latter trusted the retrieval of his fortunes to strenuous manual labour, the former to incessant quill-
driving. No man ever worked more blindly than
Richard now was doing. He was not an excellent
reporter, but that did not prevent him from writing a
guide for others; he was as full of projects as the wizard
in his most active period—not one bore the impress of
shrewd self-interest. Histories of Swindon and the
Goddards, impossible stories, imperfectly understood
antiquities and legends, furnished him with tasks that
proved mere outlets for energy.

Two things he had to learn : first, what he could write
about, and, secondly, how to write it. Without style his
knowledge was useless, because it was not special.
Naturalists had already enumerated more facts about
out-of-door life than he was master of. He was ultimately to succeed by investing homely things with

charm, and he did not yet know what he lacked. It was surprising to him that a story knocked off in a fortnight or three weeks did not fill his coffers. Yet in this unconsciousness lay his salvation, for it kept him from the fate of those feverish modern writers who go forth in search of 'style' and return with bags full of dainty phrases and curious nouns and adjectives of another world. Those affectations, useful as they are to him who has nothing to say, and whose 'art' is that of concealing intellectual barrenness or counterfeiting literature with *banalité*, would have been fatal to Jefferies. His business was not to trick out commonplace into a semblance of originality, but to reproduce for us some of the delicate and sweet delight afforded him by the simple sights and sounds of an English field. Pleasure, emotion, pain are the basis of literature, and literary art is the ability so to image one's own experience that the reader lives over again that portion of the author's life. Jefferies was no introspective analyst. With the ingenuous simplicity of a child he tells you a mallard was swimming on the lake, or a bee humming in the flowers, and you know he was pleased, and you feel as pleased yourself as if you had been with him; yet there is so little ornament it seems almost as though his writing carried conviction only by something akin to the frank sincerity of a young voice.

That is style at its highest, and it was growing in Jefferies at Swindon, but as invisibly as the Lent lily when it is pushing its way through mould and snow to meet the April sunshine. He wrote novels that publishers returned, printed books that did not pay, pursued a journalism that would not smile, and by these very hardships the circle of his activity was being narrowed to the one territory where he was master. Yet we cannot but take blame to ourselves for the excessive cruelty of his training. It almost seems as if, despite all the scoldings of all our teachers, from Samuel Johnson to Carlyle, strikingly original genius must still be prepared for the hardships meted out to a Burns or a Blake. Yet fame comes easily in these days to men of ordinary talent. If you are clever, but not too clever, if you confine your originality to conventional forms, your recognition will be instant. Jefferies established a convention. Many men are now able to make more than he did by weakly imitating his work. He won friendship and recognition and sympathy from a few individuals, but the great crowd of spectators held their thumbs down till he was killed, and then shed the tear of sentiment over his grave. But that is anticipating.

His career at Swindon was in its eager life, its impulsive mistakes, its successes and adventures, worthy of the most erratic genius whose story is told in the annals of literature. As we have seen, he had in a wild moment been a runaway from Coate. He was now to be smitten with disease, to lose employment, to be threatened with an action for debt, and to be stricken with poverty so dire that only a halfpenny remained in his purse before he was permitted to score at all in his contest with misfortune. Even in mishap, however, there was teaching and consolation. The cottagers whom he never could understand came in his illness with honey and presents, showing, if he could have seen, how no malice had edged their rough jesting about him. And he made the discovery that ' after all, books are dead; they should not be our whole study. Too much study is selfish.' That was the beginning of his emancipation, for he was to be no mere critic living on the fame of others, but one whose work was to be a record of his own experience.

For some time yet he was to flounder after many will-o'-the-wisps. Mr. Besant says in 1870, the year of the Franco-Prussian war, he had money enough to take a continental holiday, but the adventure reads almost like a repetition of his earlier escapade. It could never have occurred to any one but a child of nature. At Hastings he writes verses to the exiled Prince Imperial, and is sky-high at their being accepted We hear of him admiring the women and the wine of Brussels; and such is his eager enjoyment, we may not suspect the truth that the whole of his money is melting away. Nay, more, he had left without warning, and found himself, when he came back to Coate, like an escaped canary that after an hour's freedom among the apple-trees flies back to its cage when hungry; his father's door was closed to him, and the newspaper offices refused him admittance. First there was only two and threepence in his pocket, then only a half-penny, and how quiet and penitent he was after his escapade will appear from the following letter kindly placed in my hands by Mr. Harmer of Cirencester, to whom it was addressed :—

'COATE, *December 15th*, 1870.

'DEAR SIR,—I did not expect so kind an answer as you sent me. I wish now I had written long before. I have been engaged almost all the year trying to make some progress as an author. In the last four months I have been occupied writing a book, which Mr. Disraeli was good enough to say was on an interesting subject, and to

recommend me to send it to some publisher. So Messrs.
Smith, Elder and Co. are now considering the manuscript.
I find, however, that it is better to have some permanent
employment while making these efforts, and lately I have
done some little reporting; indeed, with a view to such
work in the future, I have carefully kept up my shorthand. I have been thinking of taking a regular situation
with the new year, and, before I apply elsewhere, I should
much like to know if there is any possibility of doing anything for you. The kind tone of your letter reminds me
that you were a most considerate employer, and if the
salary you can give me is not large, on the other hand the
work is not excessive, and there is time at one's disposal.
I frankly confess that I should much like my old place
again, and that it would be a considerable advantage to me.
I would endeavour to give satisfaction, and I think I may
say I tried to suit you while with you. I know the
neighbourhood thoroughly. Perhaps you will at least take
the idea into consideration before replying. I am aware
that what has passed is a great obstacle, but it is certain
that the knowledge I have gained of the world since then,
and the more correct light in which I now view and
value things, is the best guarantee against its recurrence.
I have enclosed a few lines of my own for the *Standard*, and
remain, yours respectfully,　　　RICHARD JEFFERIES.'

The letter from Disraeli alluded to will always be
remembered as an example of that strange and brilliant
statesman's recognition of merit. One cannot help
smiling, however, at the elation of Jefferies over it, and
at his ingenuous description of the writer as 'the man
who stands highest in our age for intellectual power.'
It will be seen that despite his struggles towards
authorship the young countryman had imbibed no
Carlylean horror of journalism. His life at present is a
hard struggle for existence, and 'Any port in a storm'
might have been his motto. Yet it would almost
appear as if some Muse sister to her who appeared in

the auld clay biggin' of Burns was warding him from
that fatal morass; or, in the matter-of-fact language of
his biographer, 'he was going to make a big mess of two
or three jobs before he really found himself.'

The *Times*, which more than once has distinguished
itself by a recognition of obscure merit, was the scene of
his first success in the eyes of a world which did not
share his own view as to the distinction of becoming
known as a writer in both Swindon papers. His letters
on the Wiltshire Labourer show his great faculty for
noting externals, but in respect to anything else are as
unsatisfactory as his novels. The lament over his
ineptitude to utilise them as an instrument for widening the cleft in his oyster of a world is I think
misplaced. In his boyish inexperience he had told
reporters to 'treat literature as a trade which, like other
trades, requires an immense amount of advertising,' but
no one shrank more fastidiously than he did from the
methods of the literary charlatan. Besides, the un-
shaken trust in himself that persisted through all his
early troubles was not founded on the hope of rising
from one point to another in journalism, but in a belief
in his capacity for accomplishing more enduring
work.

Instead of swelling the noise with puffery, according
to the terms of his own prescription—dictated less by
conviction than contempt, I fancy—he went quietly
about his work, thinking, in his inexperience perhaps,
that from this test of his quality others would guess
the power of which he was conscious. He did not
know how the world's dulness is most dense in the
presence of promise; that while the abject penny-a-
liner is paid and flattered into quackery, the solid work

of great talent is oftenest ignored, and stupidity stands
amazed or impudently jeering before those resplendent
streaks that show in the worst bunglings of genius.

Whatever kept Jefferies in Coate, however, was for
his intellectual and physical good. His courtship had
been going on for some time, and now (1874) ended
in marriage. From the neighbouring farm he took
to the old home at Coate an early playmate and a
sympathetic companion. A time was approaching
when his last farewell would be paid to it. Every
month of delay was so much more won to the making
of him. His good genius was gradually elbowing him
away from those journalistic duties of the reporter that
might eventually have made a hack or a tradesman of
him. The local paper indeed helped on his development,
for your county weekly, when it suffers from lack of
matter, is a great encourager of the descriptive article.
Many people in North Wiltshire date their remembrance of Jefferies from a series of essays on Village
Churches, for the writing of which he perambulated the
district, and there is enduring work of his to show how
deep were the impressions made. It was in autumn,
for the green yew showed its red berries through the
window, and though he does not mention Chiseldon by
name, one cannot, without thinking of its grey and
gargoyled church, read what he has to say of the elms
and beeches and the steep down, grey-mottled with
sheep. Though he had visited many another, it is
highly characteristic that the church from which he had
walked with his sweetheart on Sunday evenings, and
close to the door of which is the sleeping-place of his
forefathers, should have been most conspicuously present
in his mind. Now, too, he was beginning to practise his

craft with power—no longer dashing off novels at railway speed, and feeling astonished that they did not sell,
but slowly and carefully working at those shorter and
less ambitious efforts on which ultimately his fame was
to rest. It was by no deliberate choice he did so.
Writers fortunately raised above pecuniary cares are at
liberty to select their own ground. By examining the
causes of failure, and with leisurely determination
rectifying them, they have a chance of proving the
accuracy of their self-knowledge. A man continually
dogged by want, with the needs of a wife and children
to attend to, must push as best he may along the line of
least resistance. Jefferies wanted to write novels, but
was forced to write essays. Mr. Walter Besant and
others have, as I think unreasonably, ridiculed his
ambition. They forget that his was a slowly maturing
mind, and his early experience narrow. Scott, Fielding,
Thackeray—how many novelists there have been whose
success began at middle age!—and certainly had the
author of *Tom Jones* left nothing but his plays as little
promise would have been discerned in them as in *The
Scarlet Shawl*. A man knows himself best, and who
can say that had Jefferies lived he might not have
succeeded in romance? At forty, says M. Renan, is
time enough for a man's writing to begin, and Jefferies
died at thirty-eight. There was, as far as I can see, only
one difficult obstacle in his way, and contemporary
successes show that even it is no barrier to money-making
by romance. Almost all stories of the first rank are
full of humour. *Don Quixote* and *Gil Blas*, *Tom Jones*
and *The Antiquary*, *Pendennis* and (may I add?) *The
Master of Ballantrae*, are tinged with it. No man
indeed seems to see life clearly unless he perceives, not

only its drolleries and oddities and contradictions, but that not infrequently tears are stemmed by laughter and tragedy transposed into comedy. Jefferies did not inherit this corrective of over-seriousness, and it is not to be acquired.

On the other hand, his slightest sketches of human beings—the farmers, poachers, gamekeepers, and labourers introduced into his later works—are drawn with the same minute fidelity as his birds and plants, his talent in that respect reminding one forcibly of the better part of Emile Zola. The point is of importance, because Jefferies himself was never quite satisfied—nor are his readers—with the form circumstances obliged him to adopt. Some critics have expressed this dissatisfaction by inveighing against his tendency to catalogue, and declaring that he never rose above being a reporter. But this is a mere fumbling for the name and explanation of a fault. Obviously the sort of work done by Jefferies at Swindon, or that done by any man in his position, was a great deal more likely to develop word-spinning than catalogue, and of all the terms applicable to the defect catalogue is the least appropriate. Any ordinarily expert naturalist, set in a sunny field with pencil and notebook, could observe and make a list equal, as a list, to any of his; for he saw nothing that was not patent to every open eye. You may test the truth of that in many ways. Do you go to him or to more commonplace authors when it is desirable to obtain information or to clear up a disputed point in natural history? If his more ecstatic admirers are right, and the closeness of his observation be the crowning point of his virtues, where is the fruit of it? What has he added to this branch of science? After being neglected in his lifetime it would appear to be his fate to be misunderstood and misinterpreted now that he is dead.

His mind was of too musing and contemplative an order for him to shine with extraordinary brilliance as a mere collector of facts. The field-naturalist lives in dread lest his intellect should lose the edge of its activity. His aim is to be constantly alert, active, vigilant; if wise, he will not even smoke at his task, lest he be lulled into dream and reflection when he should only see. Jefferies to the verge of indolence was still and meditative. For his walks he did not prefer the hedgerows, meadows, and woods, teeming with life, but the bare and open downs, where the only music was made by the wind moaning through the Follies or sighing in the hollows; where a hovering kestrel or a hare limping round the shoulder of a hill were intruders in a scene otherwise empty save for the clouds whose drifting beauty was more than scientific fact to him. We hear nothing of his making botanical or other collections, though both his father and grandfather appear to have done so; of his experimenting, otherwise than as to the most effective methods of killing game. If he had a passion for information it found extremely little expression by the usual channels.

Others name him Nature's prose-poet, and in safe generalities talk of the 'interest' and 'charm' of his writings, and they certainly are happier than those who denominate him a maker of catalogues. Mr. Besant, I think, in his Eulogy slurs over his verse. 'I wonder,' he says, 'what that manuscript (his first) was. Perhaps poetry—a clever lad's first attempt at verse; there is never a clever lad who does not try his hand at verse.'

Jefferies did write poetry, and showed promise of succeeding with it, as much promise as you shall find in
the *Hours of Idleness* or the first crude flights of Lord
Tennyson.

The peculiar merit of his prose never will be understood unless we clearly apprehend the central fact by
which the magician of the fields dominated him. It was
not sport, although he knew the charm of gun and rod ; it
was not science, much as his intellect soared and
speculated. What it was he has told us himself: 'I
seem as if I could feel all the glowing life the sunshine
gives and the south wind calls to being. The endless
grass, the endless leaves, the immense strength of the
oak expanding, the unalloyed joy of finch and blackbird :
from all of these I receive a little ; each gives me something of the pure joy they gather for themselves. In
the blackbird's melody one note is mine ; in the dance
of the leaf-shadows the formed maze is for me though
the motion is theirs ; the flowers with a thousand faces
have collected the kisses of the morning. Feeling
with them, I receive some at least of their fulness of
life.'

Busy, striving, struggling, toiling, weary men seek
Nature for solace and rest, but no sooner is her invigor-
ating influence felt than they begin to desire a return
to labour. Sportsman, philosopher, student, court her
for ulterior motives. Jefferies was her disinterested lover.
It was enough for him simply to live in sun and wind,
and feel that he was one with the blowing, moving life
around him, with bursting leaf and running beast. 'The
hours when the mind is absorbed by beauty are the
only hours in which we really live,' and in those hours
when he was held as by a spell Nature poured her images

into his rich and sensuous mind. She was most prodigal and he most receptive during those happy days at Coate before he dreamed of selling this experience for bread.

In this sordid and care-stricken world not many people are capable of so detaching themselves from worldly affairs as to enter into this joy. 'No one else,' he says, 'seems to have seen the sparkle on the brook, or heard the music at the hatch, or to have felt back through the centuries; and when I try to describe these things to them they look at me with stolid incredulity.' But those who really love and appreciate his work are such as have shared, be it ever so lightly, in the intimate pleasures he has described. They may not know Coate, but memory holds the ripple and glitter of other streams, of sweet and similar music, of youthful thought and feeling gone with the fair sunsets and mysterious dusks visible to the young alone. In reading Jefferies, ghosts of dead pleasures pass in train before us. Once more the greens and yellows are as bright as they appeared to the happy excitement of youth, pictures of living animals glow again, the merry hedgerows, the stiled footpaths across the meadows, banks whereon our wild-flowers grew, early home and heath and garden come back. The very force of the egotism with which his memory recalls and his imagination bodies forth pictures deepens our interest. It is the personal feeling that raises Jefferies so far above all other writers on the open air.

Yet in the heat of our admiration there remains something of that dissatisfaction he felt with his own work, a suspicion that other poets and prose-writers, nay, even the general taste, are right in using material similar to that of Jefferies as border and background only. The exquisitely carved leaves on the walls of Melrose Abbey would not be less beautiful if separated, alike in their environment and the intention of the artist, from that building; and yet who could admire a miscellaneous and unordered heap of sculpture and pilaster, stained glass and woodwork, as much as a cathedral in which each has its well-considered place? An essay by Jefferies is a succession of fine but disconnected pictures, and is without beginning, middle, or end. In bits it is unsurpassable, as a whole it has no interest. One objects to a kind of aimlessness in it, as if the artist had no general impression on his mind. The fault seems to have been one of constitution, for his stories too suffer from the lack of any central idea or skilful grouping. Even in his descriptions he will bring before your mind's eye a single meadow, or hedgerow, or spot on the Downs, but very seldom do his eyes travel on to the wide landscape around. And as one defect leads to another, digression is an almost unavoidable consequence. A novelist eager to get his story told, or an essayist intent upon some broad effect, selects from his material such portions only as bear on his purpose. Jefferies never could withstand the temptation to make parentheses of any quite non-significant facts that occurred to him; and every introduction of this kind made his work less interesting and attractive to the multitude. Those who understand him will not find fault. If Jefferies had been different, more active and practical say, he could not have loitered in the fields so calmly and contentedly while the graving on his mind grew deeper; had he known how to invent plots and weave them into stories he could not have also made the unique addition to English literature we have had from him.

In these days every literary man has sooner or later to face the great battle of London, and Jefferies, as he found himself at last gaining position as a successful magazine writer, yielded to the attraction. It has been plaintively complained that he did so without having mastered the indispensable secret known as 'working the oracle.' Your astute young author of the modern school, and many of his still more astute seniors, have methods of widening reputation not to be learned on the Wiltshire Downs. 'Never miss an opportunity of having your name in the papers' is one of their frankly accepted rules, and as toadies and jackals are plentiful enough their success is wonderful. I would have less respect for Jefferies if he had failed to treat those base and brazen arts with haughty disdain, and it seems to me a lasting disgrace that any reason exists for the complaint of his biographer, that inattention to them was the origin of his pecuniary troubles. It is to our shame, and not his, if the manufacturer of shoddy succeeds with his puffery, and is enriched, while he who sells honestly honest goods is neglected ; and the society of authors would perform a wholesome purgation if it would brand with infamy every member known to pursue the tactics neglected by Jefferies, *i.e.* every one who 'sought to be mentioned in the papers,' or who 'courted popularity in the ways very well known to all, and commonly practised without concealment.' Then perhaps we should be spared the spectacle of neglected genius dying penniless, while notorious literary mediocrities, quacks, and humbugs, find 'the cheques come rolling in.'

Nor is it to be regretted that Richard Jefferies stood aloof from the literary society of London. It has not improved much since the days when it was an object of Thackeray's mockery and Carlyle's scorn. Most of the men who add enduring books to literature find it safer to avoid the pigmy circles from which come theories of literary art, doctrines of criticism, and other kinds of din that only confuse a man whose work lies before him. It is just because he had so little theory about his craft, and was so entirely free from the feverish self-consciousness of the typical literary man of to-day that the biography of Jefferies stands out so fresh and beautiful. For he drifted, or was driven by wind and tempest, into his haven. To change the simile what he produced was of the British public's own choosing, the only one of his wares they would buy. If he offered to write them stories, or political economy, or even religion, the answer was, ' No, we will buy little country essays, and write these you must, or starve.' To a man in that position theories of literary art might well appear a mockery.

For the neglect of Jefferies, it was not the critics but the British public itself that was to blame. When the poorly educated, inexperienced countryman was at his best, he addressed the cultured few rather than the un-learned many. To this day those who live among his own fields do not read him. Many reasons might be advanced to account for this; the most obvious of which is his impregnation with the most advanced ideas of his time. At first sight it seems strange that it should be so, and yet it was natural enough. Those writers who live in the heart of the metropolis, and who are the first to know of a new name, or a new

theory, whose daily gossip is of this remarkable book,
or that striking article, and who are continually dis-
cussing realism, romanticism, decadence, all the latest
phases of art, are out-distanced by the remote and solitary thinker who reads comparatively little, and talks
less, but who with a calm and undistracted mind works
out theory and conclusion to their logical results. The
energy of the others is wasted on the sifting of news,
the collection of facts, and the discussion of side argu-
ments; while a man wandering in the fields carries
with him and muses over only a few striking ideas.
Jefferies' love of *Faust* would show, if nothing else did,
how full he is of the modern spirit. But you see it
still more clearly in that treatment of Nature which
delights the cultivated man and is caviare to the
general. Gilbert White wrote pleasantly upon free wild
life, and is perennially popular. Izaak Walton beautifully described still nature, and is loved; but there is
something in Jefferies that is not in them, nor in any
of his predecessors. Modern discovery has given
Mother Earth a new interest, and his unconvinced
mind, reflecting the religious restlessness of his age,
grasped it as hardly any other has done. Almost unconsciously to himself, he was ever dwelling on our
relationship to drifting cloud, and waving wood, and
rippling water. The critics were not always successful
in analysing the cause of their admiration, but they
were lavish in their praise, and if he had lived only a
few years longer, the lagging crowd would have yielded
also.

It is therefore difficult to see any benefit arising out of
the removal of Jefferies from Coate to Surbiton. At
peril of his self-respect, he was debarred from adopting

what Mr. Besant, who ought to know, calls the common
devices for widening fame. The praise showered upon
him would have lost its value if he had been conscious
that even the innocent bias of friendship had interfered
with the freedom and independence of his critics. He,
whose writing seems to come from an atmosphere calm
and secluded as that of a woodland glade, could not
admit a legion of chattering—say theorists, to his sanctuary. While his health remained, however, he was
under no temptation to do this.

The closing chapter in the life of Jefferies will long
be told as one of the most heroic incidents in the sad
annals of literature. It brought into play features of
personal character that hitherto had been clouded. His
illness began in December 1881, and endured for more
than five years. Until his death actually occurred, the
outside world had known less of his personality than
that of any contemporary of equal standing. In these
times, we have small reason to complain about lack of
familiarity with our celebrities. But the gossip, the in-
terviewer, the retailer of tittle-tattle, and the paragraphist told us nothing of Jefferies. Yet his works
said plainly that he was passionate, sensuous, and
tender, that he loved to loiter, and dream, and theorise,
that he had a wild and daring fancy, a bold and specu-
lative mind, and no sense of the grotesque or laughable.
Nevertheless, he was so reserved and meditative that
his neighbours at Coate were unaware even of that.
They did not know him, and he did not know them; as
far as he was concerned, they were only 'figures in the
landscape,' or, at most, embodiments of life to be
observed and described as the birds and beasts were.
His imagination never carried him below the exterior

of human life. He minutely noted the habits, dress, food, peculiarities of speech, and action of the labourers; he did not surmise how much romance might be in their lives. They were as ignorant of all but the outward figure and clothes of him. The quiet child, the long untidy boy, the idle youth, the apparently lazy young man's figure, slowly moving over field or down by dusk or sunlight, was in each stage something out of sympathy with them, an object of gossiping, scornful pity. They judged by the simple criterion of success. He did not supplement Farmer Iden's lack of agricultural skill, or stay the coming ruin. In his self-chosen calling of reporter he achieved no tangible result. His early attempts at authorship were losing transactions as commerce. At London he did not make the literary business pay. The sensitive Jefferies knew very well the estimation in which he was held, and had, as he tells us, to endure 'the sneers and bitter taunts of so many for idleness and incapacity,' and the result was that the reserved man became even more reserved, till one of the sweetest and tenderest natures was cloaked and concealed by apparent moroseness and bad temper.

Jefferies' innate worth was unknown except to his closest friends and the students of his work. The 'boundless love' that atoned for all the faults of Burns was his too. Indeed, so perfect was this feeling, so complete the sympathy between Jefferies and Nature, that they melt into one, and you do not care to use even the word love, because it implies a distinction. It was not by the penetration of fancy that he interpreted the life of brook and flower, but because he shared it. Sunshine and wind and shower were as much to him as to them.

This kindness was not spoiled by artificial and fine-drawn scruples as to life. He shot a rabbit with as clean a conscience as that of a kestrel hawking a mouse. In a world where life is supported by the destruction of life, his mind was untroubled by those fine sentiments regarding its sacredness which fadmongers have elevated into a creed. In the course of his sporting adventures he sometimes slackened his hold of the sighted gun to admire the beauty of a pheasant or a rabbit's play; but it is as difficult to imagine him losing sport out of a false pity as to think he could ever have been a wanton destroyer. In telling you how most effectually to wring a rabbit's neck, or kill a wounded bird, he takes humanity for granted, and does not insist upon lecturing.

Jefferies I judge, from his writings, to have been a man of almost Quixotic integrity, and it is a quality, as one must sorrowfully admit, that plays into the hands of the third of the giants—disease, despair, and poverty—pitted against him. He who thrives on journals and magazines is much more comfortable without the fine honesty that prevented Jefferies from writing on what was not absolutely within his own knowledge; for it is a craft where payment is calculated on bulk more than quality. A writer in haste to be rich adopts without verification the facts of others, guesses impudently where he is ignorant, trusts to a lucky shot if in doubt, and has the knack of dressing up in several guises every idea that comes off, so that he may multiply his payment for it; and all this without barefaced plagiarism or imposture. Jefferies would not do that. His very novels are made worse than they might be from his reluctance to pass beyond the mild experience of Coate farm.

To that he joined an unbending independence and pride of spirit so robust and invincible as to recall Samuel Johnson, Carlyle, Burns, and the other indomitable heroes of letters. Of the proud reticence it inspired him with, in regard to his sickness and poverty, of the manner in which it nerved him to labour in the midst of deadly torture, how it urged him, whenever the ebbing tide of health made a fallacious break shoreward, to gallantly attempt again the retrieval of his fortunes, future historians will write as they do of Gordon at Khartoum. His resolute statement, made too with a deep and unconscious pathos, that he would sooner go to the workhouse than accept the charity of the Royal Literary Fund, is one of those things we remember with admiration, whether we agree or not with his sentiments in regard to that institution. It is sufficient to know that he honestly believed there was degradation in accepting its aid. Many a day has passed since anything more heroic was chronicled than the stubborn determination of this pained and dying man, not only to fight with his last breath, but to refuse any aid in the struggle that would at all interfere with his own self-respect. And in the quality of the work done in this agony there is the strongest evidence of his force of will. The *Pageant of Summer*, says Mr. Besant, ' was written while he was in deadly pain and torture,' and not only is it admirable throughout, but the closing pages touch the high-water mark of English prose, so perfect are they in style without a trace of gaudy ornament, so rich in the highest qualities of thought, tenderness, pathos, fancy, and speculation. It is only when the mind is excited to the highest degree compatible with controlled work, when every faculty of it is awake and on the outlook, that such writing may be produced. And the essay is not better, if so good, as that final lament over the old village, written when the flame of life was still nearer the socket. I cannot imagine what critics are driving at when, with it before them, they say Jefferies had no style. You will see in many of their own compositions matter and manner coupled like a pair of ill-matched hounds, that snap and snarl and pull in opposite directions till it is painful to watch them. The thought and expression of Jefferies are not coupled; they are fused into one, and inseparable. To so concentrate and apply the faculties of his mind, while all his body was quivering with pain, was a triumph of will such as literature had not displayed since the time of Schiller.

These latest essays I think prove something more. Up to now, Jefferies had been groping and feeling about for a medium through which to express himself. Despite much effort, the novel in his hands had failed; poetry and every other form but one had been given up. The discriminating minority of the reading public had by their encouragement said plainly that in the world of letters one small territory was his, and that there he was without a rival. Practice makes perfect in the literary as in every other art, and every new essay of Jefferies, towards the end of his life, showed some improvement on its predecessors. Crudities disappeared, the digressive tendency was held in check, and ever in brighter and truer colours did the ardent mind reproduce its own reflection of the charming objects whereon it loved to work. At last, the spellbound boy had emerged from his trance, and seized the magic wand himself. He commands it to be Spring,

and lo! a brilliant green comes on the black hedgerows,
brown bourgeons of the chestnut smile and burst into
leaf, the singing of birds and 'the sweet rush of rain is
heard,' and you feel the sun shining after it; let it be
Summer, he says, and the foliage thickens, may and
apple blossom whiten the sward, the dense trees and
bushes are populous with helpless half-fledged birds,
the corn shoots upward and is waved by the wandering
breeze; Autumn with its red berries and yellow leaves,
its fatness and its decay, its full granaries and bare
fields, and icy Winter too, came at his call.   No poet,
not Burns nor Tennyson, to say nothing of lesser men—
Cowper and Thomson for example—has had a greater
power; and prose for such a purpose is a coarser instrument than verse, in which the finer shades of meaning
may be conveyed by rhyme and rhythm as well as the
melody of words.

Experience had shown however that beyond this
power something else is necessary.   It is curious that
those who are most insistent on the sufficiency of mere
colour in paint, of style in letters, should have been
promptest to condemn Jefferies as a cataloguer who
could not generalise.   And if you study their criticisms
it will become abundantly apparent that they conjure
up ninety-nine faults that do not exist, and miss the
only one, viz., that Jefferies unconsciously to himself
began by acting on their theories.   In his final essays,
however, the vacancy to be noticed in his earlier work
has disappeared.   He had found out that the working
of a human mind—the personal element, as we say—is
to those who purchase books the highest form of art.
Jefferies had made hundreds of beautiful pictures of
country scenes, and but a few purchased them.   In his

last essays you see he had added a figure, his own, to
the landscape, and if one may judge by the frequency
with which one sees them quoted, they are the most
popular. For the reader seems always to be asking the
author, What did you think about on the Downs, or
when sheltered under an oak in the rainstorm ? Is it
with pathos or regret or sadness or hope that you recall
the summer scene so vividly ?

It is an egotist that answers, but in some forms of
art egotism is the highest quality. Jefferies failed to
describe others just because he was so intent on his own
broodings and thoughts, but when he came to paint on
the canvas his own strange and rich personality, his
passionate love of beauty and sunshine, his fiery dreams
and longings, he had imparted the finishing touch to
his art. Unfortunately, like Keats and Byron, he was
taken from us too soon. The crudities of youth were
disappearing, and false lights were ceasing to lead him
astray ; after its sluggish growth his mind was ripening
at last to its harvest-time, and the literary student is
condemned to find in him now only suggestions of what
might have been. Yet his eloquent fragments may
possibly enough live long after complete works are
forgotten. Easily made reputations easily die, and the
fiery rushing genius of to-day, swiftly and easily as he
flies up the hill of fame, discovers no rest on its summit,
but is compelled to hurry still more rapidly into the
thick irrevocable darkness on the thither side. If we
think of the number of recent reputations that have
died with the owners of them, and how many potent
names of the century are shrinking and fading, it terrifies
us from lightly assuming that this or the other poet or
novelist has really won a niche in the gallery of

immortals. Yet the unique work of Jefferies so con-
tinues to gather to itself admirers, so absolutely proves
itself inimitable that the half-educated peasant seems
in a fairer way to enduring remembrance than many
of those who rolled in wealth while he scrambled in
poverty.

II

ART AND SCENERY

(LORD TENNYSON)

HENRY VIII. called Lincolnshire 'one of the most brute and beastly (shires) of the English realm,' and it was an abhorrence to Sir Walter; yet it has produced one of the greatest Nature-lovers of the century, and has been to Lord Tennyson all that his hills were to Wordsworth, or his Borderland to Scott. Jefferies has not painted Coate nor Thoreau his Walden ponds more ardently than he has pictured its lonely moors and grey wolds and the low bleak shores of the Wash. Has he loved Lincolnshire in spite of itself, or do inspiring beauties really lurk in its levels and pastures, its gardens and orchards? It is the question you cannot help asking if ever you fare to Somersby and the landscape that will endure as long as the Laureate's verse. Here it was that he lived till he was twenty-five, that is, during the youthful period of unconscious assimilation, and here he received impressions that have remained vivid and ineffaceable in his hoar old age. Unlike his predecessor in the Laureateship, who named as he sang his lakes and hills, or Burns, whose Ayr and Nith seem as familiar and personal as Bonnie Jean or Highland Mary, Lord Tennyson has been careful not to particu-

larise. If you know Lincolnshire at all you feel,
as you read *Locksley Hall*, that the scene is a
familiar one; there is more of the country in it than
the ocean beach and the sandy ridges, the curlews and
the moorland; yet if you compare the Hall of the famous
poem with Langton Hall or that at North Somercotes
there is only such a general resemblance as exists, say,
between Ramsay of Ochtertyre and Jonathan Oldbuck.

So, too, when he sang the song of the brook, he was
not celebrating the clear and rapid streamlet that
glances past Tetford with a ripple like a smile just
breaking into laughter; but the summer setting of his
immortal burden — the fairy forelands, the sailing
blossom, the fresh wet ferns—belongs to a flat country.
What north-country poet who knows a burn as one
day a dribble of water between pool and pool in a waste
of stone and boulder, and the next as a swollen and
turbulent river, could have informed his picture with
the sunny tranquillity of Tennyson's? Looking up
from the bridge across the brook at Tetford to the low
hills where it rises, and so down to the flat meadows by
which it flows away, you recognise that the boy had
never a Tweed to rave past him over its bed of gravel,
and sing him full of dark Border romance—had no
Eildon, nor Lomond, nor any Lachin-y-Gair. No frown-
ing sea-cliff was near to teach him grandeur. Except
the parish church of Louth, there was not even any
great architecture closer than Lincoln Cathedral, and
that was some thirty miles away. Worse than all, the
country is not rich in tradition, nor in ballad, nor in
legend; it counts in its inheritance few or none of those
'old unhappy far-off things' that are the staple of a
certain type of poetry. To be exact, indeed, it is the

most prosaic shire in England, and its people the most
prosaic of Englishmen.

And yet a single view of Somersby Rectory is a more
illuminative and suggestive commentary on Lord
Tennyson's verse than you shall find in all that dreary
library of criticism, the enumeration of which fattens
the Catalogue of the British Museum. You might in
fancy have built the white walled house and its
surroundings out of the poems. Even in that desolate
season when winter lingers and spring has not yet
arrived, its seclusion and refinement, the peace and the
sweetness it suggests, seem to fit it exactly to the genius
of Tennyson. The poems are as natural to the environment as the wild snowdrops that mock the melting
snow with their numbers in the neighbouring wood, or
the whistle of the garden blackbirds, or the blackening
trains of rooks that, darkening the air with their plumes,
travel over lawn and Rectory in the February dusk.
The place could have produced no poet other than
Tennyson, and had he by ill-fate been born elsewhere,
here would have been his Eden of dream. That is not
less true because Somersby carries a suggestion of
Auburn, a mark of 'time's effacing finger' full of sadness. The Rectory alone, with its gargoyled mediæval-
looking dining-room, its long walls agleam against the
evergreens, and the lawn grass just touched with the
first brilliance of spring, looks cheerful ; for the rest, it
was not needed to write 'time passeth' on the sun-dial
in the churchyard hard by, for that legend is heavily en-
graven on the grey old grange that adjoins the Rectory,
on the church itself, and still more upon the hamlet,
shrunk into a dozen houses. In Dr. Tennyson's time the
only element of desolation was the gift of nature, where

the wold was unploughed and the marsh undrained. To-
day Thurnaby and every other waste as far as you can see
is stubbed and fruitful, and the home of the marish
mosses is turned into ploughland ; yet here as in other
districts the country folk are feverishly hurrying town-
ward, and in thorpe and hamlet many a hearth is
growing cold, many a roof-tree and gable mouldering;
the smoke curls up as it used to curl from hall and
grange ; circled by the ramage of village oak and elm the
famous Lincolnshire spires show as numerous as when

> ' Four voices of four hamlets round
>   From far and near, on mead and moor,
>   Swell out and fail, as if a door
> Were shut between me and the sound.'

But the empty cottages here and there have introduced into the pleasant scene an element of failure and
decay. In the poet's childhood there was less desertion
of country homes, though many a crumbling hall and
disappearing moat were there to suggest the sad
romantic poetry of change. Yet so closely has Lord
Tennyson been concerned with the movements and
thoughts and people of his own time that few lamenting
strains for the past are in his verse.

It is from Somersby top you obtain the widest view
of the country wherein the child first rambled, and it is
easy to imagine him—book in hand, for the young
Tennysons carried books everywhere—bird-nesting in
the wood, chasing the rabbits in the field, or startling
the shoals of minnows that people the brook. You
naturally look first for the sea, to whose sounding shore,
it is said, the lad would sometimes run hatless and
ecstatic ere he remembered he had crossed the bounds
of home. That is obviously a myth, however; sturdy

and strong as he was, he would have broken his day-dream long before he got within earshot of the Wash. Another explanation must be found, if one would fancy that of himself he said,

'Here about the beach I wander'd, nourishing a youth sublime
With the fairy tales of Science, and the long result of Time.'

Every summer his father used to carry the whole family for a month to Mablethorpe, a beautiful little watering-place near Sutton-on-Sea. The cottage where they lived, so white and oblong it might have been built in humble imitation of the Rectory, is still to be seen. When there, if you climb 'the heaped hills that mound the sea' and keep it from overflowing the level meadows behind, the favourite marine scenery of Tennyson lies all around, the dreary moorland, the barren shore,

'. . . the sandy tracts
And the hollow ocean ridges roaring into cataracts.'

As far as the eye can see, so gentle is the flat coast's slope that at ebb-tide old ocean seems wholly to have forsaken the land. So still and sombre is its beauty that at dusk when tiny songsters are twittering good-night to each other in the bents, and hardly a flash of white wings breaks the scene's grey monotony, it suggests some desolate picture in a dream where in everlasting twilight the sea's moan is answered by the gibbering of ghosts. Yet it was associated with Lord Tennyson's happy childhood, and loved by him. It was to Mablethorpe that he and his brother Charles hurried to celebrate their first literary triumph, the publication of *Poems by Two Brothers*.

To return to the top of the Wold:—You may strain your eyes to catch a glimpse from it of Lincoln Cathedral

or Boston Stump; but it is better to remark the fertility
which made Cobbett aver that 'here in Lincolnshire
are more good things than man could have had the
conscience to ask of God.' Somersby is away from the
levels, and in the prettily broken land round it every
snug farm shows a wealth of fat wethers and market-
able beeves. Ask any grumbling descendant of the
Northern Farmer, and he will confess that the land
'raäved and rembled' by his forefathers has become
splendid soil. It is a land of plenty, and yet it has
enough of wildness to enchant the lover of nature.
The drainage of the fens has depopulated them of grey
goose and cormorant and bittern and grebe, but the
creatures that flit in and out of the poems, curlew and
lark and throstle, the robin and the 'many-wintered
crow,' are singing and calling as they called and sang
seventy years ago. Many a fen-plant is gone; yet still
in May the village beauty may tell how

' The honeysuckle round the porch has wov'n its wavy bowers,
    And by the meadow trenches blow the faint sweet cuckoo flowers;
    And the wild marsh-marigold shines like fire in swamps and hollows
        gray,
    And I 'm to be Queen o' the May, mother, I 'm to be Queen o' the
        May.'

Indeed, you seem to have surprised the poet in his
workshop, and what was dreamland before seems now
to have taken visual shape. Once more the doting
grandame tells how 'Harry is in the five-acre, and
Charlie ploughing the hill,' and like her you hear them
sing to their team. Again the dying girl laments:—

' When the flowers come again, mother, beneath the waning light
    You 'll never see me more in the long gray fields at night;
    When from the dry dark wold the summer airs blow cool
        On the oat-grass and the sword-grass, and the bulrush in the pool.'

So too the 'Proputty proputty' of the farmer sounds

in the gallop of his horse's feet—three-ha'pence for twopence is the country rendering of the sound—the dying swan's coronach rises from a bed of clambering weeds, and the 'ancient homes of lord and lady' lying far and near are re-peopled with tenants of the poet's imagination.

Legend says Somersby means Summertown, and even in winter you may well believe it. Whether owing to the build of the encircling hills or the shelter of the 'immemorial elms' our poet's birthplace is a spot on which the sunshine delights to linger. Even then the meadow stretching from the other side of the highway is fresh and green; the trees though brown and bare are tall and uncontorted by the blast; the birds are babbling as blithely as if the great hawthorns were white with May, and at last you understand why it is so often summer with the poet of tilth and orchard and meadow, the singer of the dimpled brook and the garden of roses and lilies, the Laureate of the Happy Valley.

The literary history of the century seems to show that, as general education advances, culture and training are more and more demanded from the poets. It is increasingly difficult for the ploughman or artisan genius to obtain a hearing. Matthew Arnold, Mr. Swinburne, Lord Tennyson, Mr. William Morris, even Mr. Browning, are among the most scholarly of authors. The writer 'without Greek' drifts into novel-making or the drama-forms of art in which over-cultivation is fatal. To understand any poet therefore a knowledge of early training is a necessity; it is particularly so in the case of Lord Tennyson, who has reflected so accurately the changing thought of his generation that to study his verse is to follow the waves that have swept over it.

Of one of the most important portions Mr. Froude says, 'Tennyson's poems, the group of poems which closed with *In Memoriam*, became to many of us what *The Christian Year* was to orthodox churchmen.' He has never been a pioneer of thought, but he has been among the first to realise and appreciate the labours of those who have, and it is worth asking how much his delicate perception of vague intellectual movements has been due to youthful environment.

In this respect Lord Tennyson is the most fortunate poet who ever rhymed in the English tongue. He was lucky to have a home—no mere town birthplace, as was the case with Browning—but a centre for beautiful associations and enduring memories. And the domestic influence was as potent in his intellectual development as the external beauty in his love of nature. Other poets have had to struggle against adverse circumstances and unsympathetic companions and lack of opportunity; his genius was fostered and tended with as much care and solicitude as a wise gardener bestows on a favourite plant.

His father, Dr. George Clayton Tennyson, Vicar of Grimsby, as well as Rector of Somersby and Bag Enderby, was a man of vigorous *physique* and strong will as well as master of many high accomplishments. His character shows an admixture of the worldliness inherited from a legal ancestry and a devotion to mental pursuits acquired in the leisure of Bayons Manor, the residence of his father. He was a minor poet and a strong mathematician, a painter, an architect and a musician, yet was as skilful at buying and selling and bargaining as any of the hard and cautious farmers of the neighbourhood. And there is no work he

appears to have taken up with more thoroughness
than the education and training of his children.
If they were not at school he was their tutor
himself, and the neighbourhood was ransacked for
helpers and teachers. At first the Tennyson boys were
sent to the village school, where the cleverest pupils
were paid to help them on in subjects wherein they
were backward; then they were despatched to the
Grammar School at Louth; afterwards, with such
assistance as could be obtained, he prepared his own
boys for the University, which put the coping-stone to
the educational structure. The most efficacious
appliances in England were made to assist therefore in
the development of Alfred Tennyson.

Yet that was the least of it. Far more important
than any hired aid was the society of the family. Mrs.
Tennyson has not won the fame of one of those mothers
who have taken a resolute and decided part in
moulding the character and future of their children, but
no one could have exercised a kindlier and gentler
influence. Her tenderness was almost proverbial in
Somersby, and among the dwindling number of her
contemporaries there remains a memory of it as fair as
a sunset cloud that still shows streaks of light after the
sun has gone down behind the everlasting hills. She
was 'perfect music' to 'the noble words' of her
stronger and sterner husband. Mrs. Tennyson came
from the Rectory at Louth, and besides her sweetness of
disposition had the additional attractions of an artistic
temperament and much quiet and unobtrusive talent.

This well-assorted couple had a large family.
Besides the first still-born child, there were twelve
others, seven sons and five daughters, and by their

achievement afterwards we may guess their early pro-
clivities. Literary taste was not allowed to develop unconsciously at Somersby. On the contrary it was
sought for, and cherished, and criticised, and talked
about. There are families where pursuit or hobby is
hereditary. In one you have music, and the child pro-
digies begin to play and sing almost before they can
talk ; in another cricket, and the toddling three-year-
old's first feat is to wield a baby bat. Among the
Tennysons the one game, the one amusement, the one
art, was literature. Strong and healthy though the
boys were, one never hears of their skill in sport or
athletics. Out-of-doors, the Rectory children played
only such quaint and original games as could be invented from their reading. The future bard of Arthur
and Lancelot, with improvised buckler and wooden
sword, was a bold warrior in tournaments, where a heap
of stones served as castle, and happy laughing sisters
of seven or eight were the Elaine, Lynette, and Guin-
evere of his fancy. Indoors the eternal game was to
play at being authors. Each submitted his little tale
or essay to the criticism of the rest, Alfred distin-
guishing himself by the composition of an interminable
story that it took days to read. But in that period his
achievement appears to have been the object of
mockery rather than of hope, though the grandfather,
who after listening to some of his early verses, gave
him half-a-sovereign, with the remark that it was the
first and would be the last payment of his pen, cuts an
unexpected figure now, his one title to fame being this
idle jest.

The reading of the boys was however a more important part of their training than those early attempts at

composition, and how extensive this was it is now easy to see. We have Lord Tennyson's own record of his childish adoration of Byron, and how at fifteen that poet's death fell upon him with the force of a calamity. He devoured Scott while Sir Walter still was fighting the melancholy battle of his last years; Virgil's stately measure was studied, and the prose of Addison and Cicero, and the remote gods of Lucretius were becoming as familiar as the epic of Milton, while hours were idled away over the literature of the time, much of which is already dead.

Yet the children did not become premature bookworms. There was no forced study of standard authors, but as free a roving over the fields of literature as there was over fen and wold. A fine liberty was allowed them to graze where they would, and thus the mind of Alfred was never unhealthily stimulated by artificial means, but was allowed to grow naturally. All that Dr. Tennyson did was to surround his children with healthy mental food, and gently train their inclinations towards it; at the same time securing such an amount of schoolmastering as was essential to the full understanding of books.

In a recent volume of memoirs it has been asserted that indolence was a family trait of the Tennysons, and one feels sure that it must have been so; for the love of idleness must have been strong in him who sang

'Surely, surely, slumber is more sweet than toil, the shore
Than labour in the deep mid-ocean, wind and wave and oar.'

No man of an active, stirring, restless temperament may ever know much of nature. It is impossible for him to be out of doors without doing something; and

let him angle, or shoot, or hunt, let him be an ornitho-
logist, a botanist, or any other kind of scientific man,
and the Goddess of the open air never will be revealed
to him. For she is a jealous mistress, and will brook
no rival. Laziness has been the reproach of her
dearest modern lovers—of Thomson, and Jefferies, and
Thoreau—as well as of Tennyson. It means that a
man deeply to feel her influence must be able to rest
in 'dreamful ease,' unstirred by any inward monition
to be active, any desire or command to labour, any
wish to profit or advantage himself; living in breeze
and sunlight the life of an unconscious flower. The
stone is still shown in the ruins of Melrose where Sir
Walter would sit idle for hours, and the Hermit of
Walden has told how sometimes forgetting his beans
and his ponds he has sat musing at his cottage door
from the first faint flare of day till the west was red
with the sunset. In these idle and precious hours, rich
thoughts, great and vague, appear and disappear and are
the stuff out of which, in the energetic reaction that
follows, when the activity of genius is as remarkable as
its previous lethargy, are fashioned those creations that
become a part of the national life. For as names and
facts apparently forgotten will return under stress of
mental excitement, so dead dream and reverie yield
their treasures when the artist is in real need of them.
And the patriarchal poet over the chasm of half a century and more still draws upon a storehouse of scene
and fancy unwittingly garnered in boyhood.

As Alfred Tennyson grew up he still was circled by
helping influence. In his brother, Charles, he had a
companion such as it is seldom the luck of a young
writer to possess; one whose gentle disposition won the

reward of general love ; and whose more quickly ripened, though, as was ultimately to be proved, less powerful poetic talents gave him the lead of his brother's slowly ripening mind. The kindred tastes of the two acted and reacted upon one another. At Cambridge the future laureate was equally fortunate. Arthur Hallam also was scholar and poet after his own heart, and he was but one of a succession of brilliant friends.

It may well be asked, therefore, if in the long line of English poets from Chaucer onwards there is one who has enjoyed a fuller combination of happy and favouring circumstances than Lord Tennyson. Contrast his fair home with the town hovels or peasants' huts from which other bards have sprung, his cultivated and clever parents with relatives such as those of Robert Fergusson, his tranquil life with the struggle and storm of men like Byron and Shelley, the number of appreciative and sympathetic friends in his youth with the solitary fight so often maintained in the field of letters, and even then you but faintly realise how well he was trained and equipped for the battle. The victories he has won have not been of that startling kind, where the shieldless and unbucklered warrior rushes into the fray with the first rude weapon he can lay hands on, and by pure strength of arm scatters the foe. He has ridden forth like a knight armed *cap-à-pie*, his sword of Milan steel, not an unsound link in his coat of mail, not David with his sling, but Arthur with the brand Excalibur as well as his valour.

But this in no wise detracts from the honour of his achievement. If the verse is immortal, it is of comparatively small importance whether the maker framed it at the plough-tail, or in a luxurious study, whether the author's career was even and quiet or passionate and sorrowful.

> ' Win but the race—
> Who shall object " He tossed three winecups off,
> And, just at starting, Lilith kissed his lips " ? '

Nevertheless, the knowledge of an author's position and point of view, his character and training and accoutrements, is more helpful to a full appreciation of his work than the most subtle analysis or record of critical opinion. A man and his work are parts of the same, and throw light one upon the other. If by careful study of a writer's character and early life we are able to define the plot of ground whereon he is best qualified to labour, we shall, by knowing exactly what to expect and what not to expect in his pages, be saved much disappointment and irritation.

Nearly all modern poets have been writers of criticism. If we read Goethe or Wordsworth or Coleridge, Matthew Arnold or Mr. Swinburne we have the means in each case of applying the author's own tests and theories to his performance. Lord Tennyson has furnished us with no similar aid. The garrulous memoirists of the past quarter of a century have recorded scraps of his conversation, and a few of his letters have accidentally come to light, but beyond these there is nothing to explain his work save that work itself.

Like the rest he has often been falsely praised, especially by those who exalt him as the one consummate literary artist of his time. The description is superficial and inaccurate. Its meaning is simply that in contrast to Carlyle, for example, whose 'first and last secret of *Kunst* was to get a thorough intelligence of the fact to be painted,' Lord Tennyson's anxiety is

about the painting. No one is more particular about
detail than he; not Virgil himself who

> 'Would write ten lines, they say,
> At dawn, and lavish all the golden day
> To make them wealthier in his reader's eyes,'

polished and chiselled more industriously. From the
perfect accuracy with which word and thought are
mated you may see that Flaubert's solicitude about
expression was not greater than that of the poet. Not
only so, but every rhythm and rhyme, cadence, phrase,
and stop is so cunningly arranged that the sound falls
on your ear like music, and yet far from drowning the
sense delivers it more clearly than the clearest prose.

There are subtler qualities even than these to account
for the common acceptation of him by critics as the
artist of his time; and none is more striking than his
treatment of Nature. It is probable that, like Carlyle,
he learned a horror of view hunting from the profusion
of descriptions current about the time when he began
to write. At all events he invariably accords the
highest place to a dominant human interest. What
poet has ever indulged in fewer addresses to hill, lake,
and river than he? Never either directly or indirectly
has he advanced any claim to be what in an obsolescent
style of criticism is called an interpreter of Nature;
albeit his love of her finds outlet in close observation,
and his admiration in short incidental descriptions and
metaphors, the like of which for vivid illustration is
not to be found in any other chapter of English
literature. Is it possible to reproduce the feeling of a
lakeside more perfectly than in these two lines—

> 'I heard the ripple washing on the reeds
> And the wild water lapping on the crag'?

Yet passages equally graphic literally abound in the poems. Some perhaps have been jotted down in later wanderings as they occurred or were suggested; but I am convinced that the most forcible and touching are memories of the boy's loitering in the long grey fields of Lincolnshire, or of his playing between the sun and moon upon the shore at Mablethorpe. The perfect craftsmanship with which they are woven in is a cause of astonishment to those minor bards who, if they hit upon a scenic phrase, use it so awkwardly you know at once the rest is mere embroidery to it.

Nevertheless, unless we are to accept the opinion of Thoreau that Artist and Man of Genius are opposite terms, these accomplishments do not carry Lord Tennyson beyond the threshold of art. They fulfil all that is required by the definition of M. Guy de Maupassant, but Sir Walter Scott, the greatest artist of the century, not only was without them, but held an over-elaboration of style, even too much attention to it, to be pernicious. You see in M. de Maupassant himself that, although he is a hot devotee of art for art's sake, and a writer of such a French style as is a pleasure to read, he is a dull and prolix novelist, because he has no command of the supreme style that belongs to form that is in itself in fact creative imagination.

In a lesser degree the same thing is true of Tennyson. His poems are exquisite in detail but faulty in design. Most of the stories of his epic and ballads were supplied to him, and alike in his most ambitious and his simplest work the reader's interest is decreased by a lack of logical arrangement and dramatic finish. *In Memoriam* is shapelessly built; the *May Queen* a play upon an overworn bit of sentiment; and you may hardly read

Locksley Hall (the first I mean) without smiling at lines such as these—

> 'Is it well to wish thee happy?—having known me—to decline
> On a range of lower feelings and a narrower heart than mine.'

Lord Tennyson's pure and living flowers do not sprout from the bush; they are trailers and climbers twined round a dead and artificial stem. Even in *Maud* and the *Princess* the awkward and weak construction is a drawback to a full appreciation of their unforgettable passages. If he tell a story it is sure to lack plot; if he be descriptive or didactic or elegiac it is without the clever arrangement and logical drama that should hold the attention of the reader. And again, when he deals with the ordinary work-a-day struggles of life it is felt at once that he is merely a spectator. It has been said by a well-known critic that the *dramatis personæ* of his monologues are creations to be ranked with those of Shakespeare and Scott, that there you see and feel a great dramatic power never expressed in his plays. That is as great a mistake as it is to rest Lord Tennyson's fame on his being an artist. When has he painted a village beauty or a farmer? He deals only with a mood of each. You hear the clever laughter of the Rectory ringing with the 'Proputty proputty' of the horse's feet, but there is no smile on the rider's face. And it will be found elsewhere that though the lyrist finds as appropriate a lament for the dying May Queen as he did for the dying swan, it still expresses but one emotion. A lover's cry of indignation, an aged woman's wail over the past, are not in themselves character creations. The essence of drama is action, and till we have seen a youth 'sighing like a furnace,' laughing with joy and happy with hope, as well as broken by

despair, we do not know him. It is not Lord Tennyson's
gift to exhibit full and rounded pictures of men, and
Carlyle was not far wrong when he said that even the
Idylls were 'lollipops.' We shall admire him neither
wisely nor well till we have disposed of the many idle
reasons for doing so advanced by foolish or ecstatic
persons. For that blind world of criticism that stones
the prophets, if the prophets conquer at last, remains
still blind to merit, but, being now compelled to worship,
worships defect.

Lord Tennyson's claim to immortality may perhaps
ultimately rest on his jewelled speech; his present
popularity is due to his being the voice of his time.
'A work of genius,' says Nathaniel Hawthorne, 'is but
the newspaper of a century or perhaps of a hundred
centuries,' and this is peculiarly true of our greatest
Victorian poet. It has been fabled of an instrument
that it will make you hear how all potent noises still
circle the earth in faint vibrations; Miriam's triumphant
song and the battle-cry of Hector, David's harp-note
and the tramp of Cæsar's legions. Our poet's magical
gift is almost as wonderful. It has not been his
part to fight the hard, uphill battle of life, to drink
deeply of its goblet, to feel the pathos, the humour, and
the fancy of living, or to build from such experience
new worlds tenanted by men and women full of love
and strife and death, but he has lived the other life of
his time. He has an ear-trumpet that has caught every
indication of the intellectual movements of the century.
That is what he was prepared for by birth and education.

Lord Tennyson's poetry is the newspaper of his era,
and he the supreme journalist of the time. It is not

that he has been the mere reporter or chronicler of
passing events, but he has been an assiduous com-
mentator on them. He has filled his place without
aspiring to leadership. To that extent Mr. Browning
took a more decided part. No man in England has
kept more abreast of scientific discovery than he, but
although he has written the Darwinians' creed so
perfectly it has been accepted by them, he has not
emulated Goethe by assuming a place among its students
and exponents. He has not, as Victor Hugo did, taken
an active share in politics, yet no journalist or party
writer has given more brilliant expression to changing
aspirations and thoughts and ideals. His first *Locksley
Hall* was the Nicene Creed of a party. On how many
platforms have the orators found that the poet had
expressed their inmost thought and desire! And the
spirit of the nineteenth century seems to thrill in such
lines as :—

'Men, my brothers, men, the workers, ever reaping something new,
   That which they have done but earnest of the things that they
      shall do.'

Yet the same pen that wrote the cosmopolitan glorifica-
tion of 'the Parliament of man, the federation of the
world,' responds in an altered mood with a ' Britons, hold
your own.' Where again is the endless woman's question
discussed to more purpose than in the *Princess*? It is
not so much in set pieces, however, as in casual allusion
and reference occurring in every part of the poems that
you learn how attentive Lord Tennyson has been to the
political voices of his time. You find him on the crest
of every wave of great sentiment. He has chanted war
songs to England and played a requiem to her heroes;
he has recited like none other the praises of her Queen,

and there is hardly a great event in her reign unsung by him.

The years of his life have coincided with a period of stormy controversy in religion, of extraordinary discovery in science, of intellectual revolution in modes of thought, and into his ear, as if it were some fairy echoing cavern, have the voices been poured to be fluted back in music. Essayist, novel-writer, and playwright have striven to float themselves on some eddy or stream of the ebbing and flowing spiritual tide of their time; he has lived in the very centre of the flood. Whatever the men of his generation have feared or hoped or desired—their feeblest as their boldest doubts and hesitations—his poems have expressed and reflected as a moorland lake that mirrors yet blends and softens into picture blue sky and grey hill, the purple heather and the gnarled dark-green pines.

It has been the true cause of his popularity, yet it suggests its evanescence. We know that the prophecy in the following lines was a living belief when they were written, but is dead to us now, and will be without commentary meaningless to our grandchildren :—

'For I dipped into the future, far as human eye could see,
Saw the vision of the world, and all the wonder that would be :
Saw the heavens fill with commerce, argosies of magic sails,
Pilots of the purple twilight, dropping down with costly bales :
Heard the heavens fill with shouting, and there rained a ghastly dew
From the nations, airy navies grappling in the central blue.'

A writer already quoted says, 'Thoughts grow mouldy. What was good and nourishing food for one generation affords no sustenance for the next.' Lord Tennyson has so absolutely lived the spiritual life of his time that one doubts whether his work will interest the new comer. The struggle for existence has only changed in form since the *Odyssey* was written, and any true picture of its aspects hardly depends on time for acceptance, but thought is forever changing. Just as the ablest political speeches are unreadable as soon as the circumstances that gave them birth are forgotten; as a sermon hinged upon a passing form of unbelief is dying when it is uttered, even if the author be a Jeremy Taylor, a Chalmers, or an Edward Irving; as 'leading' and magazine articles have an existence commensurate only with the importance of the subject dealt with, and for the most part are dead matter before the next number comes out, so it is possible enough that poetry which has won acceptance through its permeation by the spirit of the time when it was written may fail to meet the demands of those who are coming. It were rash to prophesy, and yet is it probable that the religious question will for ever tremble on the balance, that the Darwinian cosmogony will produce no general and definite effect on belief, that opinion will always sway between materialism and its opposite? Poetry that is a brief epitome of the intellectual mutations of the century depends for its life on the doubting hearts of a generation bewildered by new discoveries, the true tendencies of which have not yet emerged from the misty region of blind surmise and vague speculation.

Even in that case, however, there will remain some deathless fragments. As long as there is strife and toil there will be intervals in strenuous life when the eagerness for battle is replaced by the rich indolence of those who

'. . . Sat them down upon the yellow sand
Between the sun and moon upon the shore.'

It is fabled of ancient magic that the adept would figure you in a water-filled chalice what you wished to see. Such a vessel is Lord Tennyson's poetry. Look into it and a procession of sweet familiar scenes, not faint and distant, but clear and vivid as well-coloured painting, passes before your eyes. It pleases, but not because the silence of the hills speaks of the Divine. The woods are unpeopled of faun and dryad and satyr. Pan no longer haunts beck or river. If beyond the inscrutable beauty that flashes and fades there is another and deeper mystery, it is still the primeval wonder of Jefferies, the insoluble problem of consciousness. 'It was all mine,' exclaimed the essayist in his own person and the poet through his characters seems to add, 'the glory of leaf and flower and sunshine was in me, yet I pass and the spring sun still calls the lark to sing at the very doorway of heaven; odorous summer, with her laughing cornfields, musical autumn, shaking red apple and berry to her piping, and winter, the father of rest, like figures in an eternal dance, pace onward before other spectators.' The mysticism of English poetry, driven from every other stronghold, still finds in that fact an impregnable refuge.

III

THE PHILOSOPHY OF IDLENESS

(HENRY DAVID THOREAU)

THE mathematical cast of Thoreau's mind expressed, as
Emerson says, in his 'powerful arithmetic,' skill in
mensuration, and a clear-cut style of thought and
writing, suggests a simile to describe the experiment of
his life. I figure him as a young algebraist confronted
with one of those huge fractions—to the uninitiated
eye a confused mass of cubes, squares, roots, numerators,
and denominators—that the late Mr. Todhunter loved
to invent for pupils to simplify. Unmanageable as it
looks, the complicated array of signs means no more
than the $a+b$ or $x-y$ into which it may be resolved.
At the beginning of his manhood Thoreau looked out
with independent eyes on the problem of living, and
found it only a vast exaggeration of the schoolboy's
task. 'By the sweat of thy brow shalt thou earn bread'
was the simple primitive curse to which the modern
man had added 'and fame and riches and pleasure.'
Yet in the strife, glory, labour, wealth and enjoyment
are subjected to so many minglings, divisions and
imitations that it requires a vigorous intellectual
effort to discover the elementary factors of the situation. Fame it was comparatively easy to eliminate from
66

the calculation, since, except as the bringer of power and money, it is of decreasing consequence to an age living only in the present. 'What matter whether they talk of or forget me when I am dead' is an obvious postulate to the creed that oblivion is better than any memory.

Of wealth is it not still true that 'whoso increaseth riches increaseth sorrow'? All the gold of the Indies can do no more than provide you with food and raiment and houseroom. The delicate dishes of the *gourmet*, the dandy's rich dress, and the Sybarite's down need no long accumulation for their purchase; and if your tastes are simple, if you are as comfortable in corduroy as in velvet, if garden vegetables and broiled fish are as pleasing to your palate as venison and turtle soup, there is the less reason to toil and save. An epicure is the bondman of his senses, and every refinement of appetite is a demand for more labour. If I can pleasurably appease my hunger with a handful of pulse, I am richer than he whose fastidious stomach demands soup and game, wine and sweets. And other pleasures are purest and fullest in their elementary form. The most brilliant orchestra is only a complication of the music made by the wind and the wild birds, and the canopied bed yields no deeper sleep than the rudest shakedown. In the mazy pageant of life, a bedizened flaunting Pleasure, her withered skin plastered with rouge, her poor form disguised with rich mantle and wrappage, has a crowd of wooers, while her ever-young sister of the groves, innocence in her eyes, glowing health on her cheeks, a natural red on her unkissed pouting lips, goes a-nutting in the September woods, or laughs while blustering March seizes her by the gown, and hardly a suitor fares in search of her.

But if the facts were otherwise, if luxury really held a sweet and peculiar joy of its own, the question would still remain as to whether it is worth the price asked for it. The labour we delight in is seldom the labour that brings wealth. History is strewn with the names of men chastised with poverty for resolutely refusing to do anything undictated by their own talents and inclinations. We do not search for millionaires among the most hard-working of men, the reformers, thinkers, poets, philosophers, artists, and statesmen, who unremittingly and ungrudgingly have with will and fervour devoted themselves to an art or an idea, but among tricky speculators and men who would laugh to scorn the suggestion that they had ever done a handsturn at anything except for wages. They, the wealthiest and most powerful, are but hired men. And it is really worth considering whether a few more delicacies at table, an extra coverlet at night, and an occasional concert form an adequate return for a lifetime's drudgery. For the deepest joys of life are neither to be bought nor sold. To one man they arrive as accompaniment and reward of victorious endeavour; to another with revelation and beauty and vision ; but for Thoreau they lurked in the clear depths of Walden Pond, they came with the sunbeams that fell on his hermitage, they wandered with him on the banks of the Musquetakid, and followed where arrowhead and broken spear told how Sioux and Comanche brave had battled under the greenwood. He tried to act up to his own injunction, ' Love your life poor as it is . . . The setting sun is reflected from the windows of the almshouse as brightly as from the rich man's abode ; the snow melts before its door as early in the spring.'

It needs but a glance at his biography to show that Thoreau's reduction of the numerator and denominator of life arose from no slothfulness of disposition, such as dwelt in him, 'more fat than bard beseems,' whose fancy built him a ' Castle of Indolence '; nor did he envy the furry sleeper who escapes the winter's rages in the rocking cradle of the trees, sinking into deeper forgetfulness with every new burst of storm. He had gentle blood in his veins, and possibly enough a far-off Viking strain, but his father was a thrifty, industrious, and rather unfortunate pencil-maker, and if genius had been expected to develop in the family, it might reasonably have been looked for in an impersonation of push, vigour, and worldly audacity. There was an almost Scottish ambition manifested in the united efforts of the family to secure for their rising hope all the advantages of a good education.

Henry Thoreau, in fact, was almost as fortunate as Lord Tennyson in his home and childhood. The scenery about his birthplace had many of the finest characteristics belonging to our midland shires—broad meadows, swelling woodland heights, a slow deep river, and several beautiful ponds. The poorest child-lover of nature might wander at will among the trees without meeting the 'Trespassers will be prosecuted' that is ubiquitous in England. If we can picture Thoreau a barefooted boy of six driving his mother's cows to pasture, or with the manliness of ten shouldering gun or angle, and roaming the forsaken Indian hunting grounds, we may know the earliness and depth of his associations. He learned to love wood and water like an aboriginal. But simultaneously he was being effectively introduced to the world of books at the famous

Concord Academy, where he imbibed a taste for the classics that was the secondary passion of his life. When at sixteen his course there was ended, the taciturn father, a sister who had saved a trifle at school-keeping, and possibly another friend or two, combined their means to send him to Harvard University, where by dint of plain living and vacation toil he managed to meet the expenses with these small means. All the funds that could be eked together left him still a poor scholar, one who, even if he had so desired, was prohibited from sharing in the expensive pleasures of his companions. The native independence and seclusion of his character were deepened by a forced abstinence from the sowing of wild oats usual at this period of life, and the plain living that was partly compulsory grew into a habit. But he was not wholly a gainer. He who drinks deeply of every chalice life has to offer, who has looked on the wine when it is red, and lived in the light of a woman's eye, who has been eager in wanton frolic, and who has opened the window shutter to let the first sunbeams fall on the smoke of a carousal, has had the chance of learning more philosophy than is to be found in any cloistered and unbreathed virtue. The shepherd's praise of Pan is less convincing than that of Jaques and the banished duke. And of people, he was not even observant, for a 'reverie hung always about him, and not so loosely as the odd garments which the pious household care furnished.'

There was another feature of his career at college that I think ultimately proved an obstacle to his full and natural development. It seems ungracious to say anything against the kindly interest taken by Emerson in his career, and yet it was rather an impediment than an aid. The new-comer to Concord, who had learned something of the boy's promise from Dr. Ripley, seems to have tried to act Providence to the youthful Thoreau, and of course the older and greatly distinguished man easily obtained an influence over his *protégé.* If they had only known it, the talents of the two lay in quite different fields, and more and more we see as time passes the reflected Transcendentalism of Thoreau fall into oblivion, followed as some think by that of Emerson also, while the study of nature, that was his own peculiar sphere, wins a wider and fuller appreciation.

If, however, we consider Emerson's disinterested and effective zeal for his disciple, it is obvious that the latter would scarcely have been mortal had he resisted. At college Thoreau probably enough nursed plans and ideals of his own, but however dogmatic he might be by temperament he had neither experience nor achievement to warrant him in steering an independent course. No scholastic or other distinction had come within his grasp, and it was doubtful if on leaving Harvard he was the possessor of any means of earning a livelihood. His pleasures had been to study the older English poets, and to wander alone by field and forest, and it had not occurred to him that a way to make money is by coining your enjoyment. Instead of rebelling against the straitness of his circumstances, or being thereby fired to more strenuous endeavour, he had cleared his mind of any pecuniary desire or ambition that might have glimmered there. It is not unusual for generous and brilliant youth, eagerly panting for a place on the battlefield, to deride and contemn money, except as the accident of fame, or the key to power ; but the problem

that was to engross so much of Thoreau's attention was
obscuring everything else. ' What is life ?' he asked, and,
as keenly as a naturalist studies a new specimen, he
turned to himself for an answer. There were two
Thoreaus; one who lived and dreamed, another whose
business was to weigh and interpret the actions of the
other. At seventeen he already kept ' a journal or
record of thoughts, feelings, studies and daily experience,' and periodically settled accounts with his mind.
Like Jefferies, he loved the reverie begotten of clouds,
and the sparkle of morning sunbeams on water, and
Coate was not loved more ardently than Concord.

Even a budding philosopher, however, must con-
descend to earn a living, and on leaving the University
at the age of twenty, Thoreau, like many another youth
of promise, found himself compelled in default of anything else to resort to pedagogy. How, with a testi-
monial from Emerson in his pocket, he fruitlessly
searched Maine for employment and came back to
teach in the Concord Academy are insignificant facts
in his career. He ' did not teach for the good of his
fellow-men, but simply for a livelihood,' and after a
year or two of maturing thought gerund-grinding was
abandoned.

It is like running over a list of dates in history to
mention that between the latter event and his removal
to the woodland hut in Walden he worked with the
family at pencil making, was an occasional land
surveyor, wrote for the *Dial*, lived with Emerson, held
a tutorship in Staten Island, went to New York, and
formed a friendship with Horace Greeley and others.
Of far more interest is it to piece together the hints of
that fiery experience that changed the dull and dream-

ing student of Harvard into the vigorous, self-assertive and somewhat cynical hermit of Walden. The making of Thoreau was a hard, cruel, and embittering process; for underneath this quiet record of events there was a deeper story of struggle and self-denial and flashing visions of happiness and the greetings of death and sorrow. One may see by his own calculations and by his wincing under reproach that his stoical course was not pursued without many a desperate search for another. Whether he should not, like other common mortals, steadfastly take up and pursue a trade instead of living from hand to mouth by casual and erratic labour was a graver question than readers of *Walden* might fancy. And the final answer was probably due as much to the painful ending of his romantic love-story as to meditation. Suppose he had courted and won instead of surrendering to his brother the girl flame of his youth, what then would have become of his philosophy? Thoreau married, Thoreau the father of a family, Thoreau with doctors' and tradesmen's bills to meet would not have been the Thoreau we know. Even if he had carried his household to the woods there would have been an end of his forty-six weeks of vacation. He who for a brief interval has built in his fancy a home for his love and his children, then finds the picture blurred, the palace shattered, may be stronger but will also be sterner for the sacrifice, even if it be of his own unsolicited making. And if the pursuits of mankind seemed previously dictated by a thirst for feverish unreal joys, or the accumulation of those 'treasures on earth where thieves break through and steal,' they are not likely to gain afterwards in dignity or attraction.

He made acquaintance with a still deeper grief than that of self-renunciation. 'A man,' he said, ' can attend but one funeral in the course of his life, can behold but one corpse,' and elsewhere he reflects that a part of us dies with the death of each of our friends. Thoreau's attachment to his brother John was as that of David for Jonathan. With him he had watched ' the fabulous river men ' in their barges pass up the slow Musquetakid, with him he had laboured in school and spent that famous holiday on the Merrimac ; the two had the same friends and loved the same places ; it was for John's sake he had laid aside his hope of marriage ; and the worthy object of all this affection returned it with interest. But Death takes no account of the closest human ties, and the loss of John in the prime of his life brought Henry face to face with the darkest form of sorrow. It was something he could hardly bear to think of or allude to for the rest of his life, and he held the name of the dead so sacred that in the *Week* he never tells who his companion was. In the portrait of his mind done unconsciously in subsequent writings the scars of these wounds are easily discerned.

Other troubles had come upon him before he went to Walden. He had been perplexed with religious doubts, and had wrenched himself away from the congregation of his old friend Dr. Ripley, and the absence of any task he loved, of any occupation that would yield him at once bread and solace, gradually strengthened his doubts of the value of any common career. Since his prostration at Harvard, too, he had, despite the prodigious activity that surprised those who regarded his narrow chest and stooping shoulders, been troubled with symptoms of illness ; and the din of battle has

less attraction for the weakly than the strong. In more
senses than one he was but

> '. . . a parcel of vain strivings, tied
> By a chance bond together.'

Last of all, this typical example of perplexed, suffering,
and disappointed humanity was beat upon by the rays
of American Transcendentalism. Thoreau had come to
know Emerson personally at the age of twenty, and in
1841, after his school-keeping and pencil-making experience, became an inmate of the philosopher's household, where ' he was to have his board, etc., for what he
chose to do.' Like many men of austere and secluded
habits, his soul was as wax to the impressions of those
he admitted to intimacy, and in his style of thought,
and even in the expression of his features, he soon began
to reflect Emerson. A story is told on the authority of
Mr. Sanborn of a person who on seeing him at Cambridge cried, ' Look at Thoreau yonder, he is getting up
a nose like Emerson's ' ; and Mr. Haskins records that
in his manners, in the tones of his voice, in his modes
of expression, even in the hesitations and pauses of his
speech, he had become the counterpart of Mr. Emerson.
' Thoreau's college voice bore no resemblance to Mr.
Emerson's, and was so familiar to my ear that I could
have readily identified him by it in the dark. I was so
much struck by the change that I took the opportunity,
as they sat near together talking, of listening with
closed eyes, and I was unable to determine with certainty
which was speaking.' These physical phenomena were
external signs of an intellectual imitation. Among the
circle of mystics that gathered in Concord, the common
dialect—a watered Carlylese—proclaimed how the
dominant personality gave a keynote to the others.

Even in describing the Bachelor of Nature, as he was christened, all his friends, with the exception of Nathaniel Hawthorne, revel in vague and extravagant phrases. 'He sets no limit to his life nor to the invasions of Nature,' writes Margaret Fuller, and beseeches that he may be left 'at peace amid his native sorrows.' Emerson tells Carlyle 'he is a noble manly youth full of melodies and inventions,' and these are the most definite and least extravagant accounts of him. But if Hawthorne's picture be a true one of 'the hobgoblins of flesh and blood' who in burlesque wisdom brought their new thoughts to be tested at Concord, 'as the finder of a glittering gem hastens to a lapidary,' one can account for the stilts and inflation.

Thoreau at the core might remain unaffected, but his sum in algebra did not look easier when the simple elements of life and death were bulked out by the immensities and eternities, the everlasting something, the roaring loom of Time, and other unmanageable factors known of the Transcendentalist. Before his era men who were marked out to be students of nature had forsaken civilisation and frugally pursued their quest in wood and glen, living their appointed lives and accomplishing the tasks nearest them. 'I was,' he says, 'self-appointed inspector of snow-storms and rain-storms, and did my duty faithfully; surveyor if not of highways then of forest paths.' So too was Richard Jefferies, and he likewise discovered that his fellow citizens were not very willing to pay for such work. At that period, however, both in England and America there was prevalent among certain thinkers a belief that every man ought to do some labour with his hands. 'Can they plough,' asked Mr. Ruskin a quarter of a century later concerning our youths, ' can they sow, can they plant at the right time or build with a steady hand?' At Brook Farm, Fruitlands, and other places, experiments in this ideal life, where thought and labour were mingled in equal quantities, had been tried, but had not commended themselves to the judgment of Emerson or Thoreau. The exile of Thoreau, however, was in a measure prompted by this as well as by his love of Nature.

Yet there were further and perhaps deeper influences at work. In the early ages of Christianity it was not uncommon for one who during a brief season had made a brave show in the World's Fair, weary, heart-sore, and disappointed, to withdraw from the turmoil, and from solitary cave or rough woodland hut look forth on the circling processional seasons, till the red and green became dim to his ageing eyes and death seized him and he was resolved into dust again. People glibly condemn all that now, saying that the world was none the better for the regular orisons, the quavering chant that mingled with the morning song of birds grown fearless of a companion who lived on roots and pulse rather than slay them. But the anchorite's rebellion against action was not always due to a creed. Otherwise there would have been no cells without crucifix and rosary, none in times anterior to that dawning whereon the herdsmen of Bethlehem first heard the natal song of Christ, none in lands deaf to the echo of that melody. If men had not sometimes longed to enjoy life without the labour and sorrow of living, poets never would have fabled of lotos and nepenthe; if they did not desire to turn their backs on all useless, aimless strife, why all their contrivances to secure a transient and partial oblivion? If eagerness for battle be not balanced by a desire of peace, how is it that nearly all the victims of death give him welcome at last?

Thoreau was no Stylites, but a trace of Simeon's spirit mingled with other causes of his asceticism. Solitude was in a measure sweetened to him by adversity, and retirement afforded him a means of examining life from a detached and independent stand-point. It had been quite possible to approach the study by another method and take life at its largest. But circumstances forbade him to inquire what it looks like after you have plunged headlong into its whirling eddies. He could not analyse the joys of strenuous labour, of luxury and travel, of love and battle, of riot and laughter; hardly those of artistic and literary triumph. Nevertheless, by eliminating all that was unessential, he reduced it to its simplest elements, brought it within the narrowest compass, or as he himself puts it, 'I wanted to live deep and suck out all the marrow of life, to live so sturdily and Spartan-like as to put to rout all that was not life, to cut a broad swathe and shave close, to drive life into a corner, and reduce it to its lowest terms, and if it be proved to be mean, why then to get the whole and genuine meanness of it, and publish its meanness to the world.'

If complicated and artificial pleasures were struck out, so also was unnecessary pain. Thoreau represents himself as an epicure rather than as an ascetic. His aim was not to mortify the flesh but to extract from existence the maximum of enjoyment. Even his vegetarianism was dictated by the desire of health as much as pity for the animals. Yet his motives here as elsewhere were mixed. He kept the natural man's instinct for sport sternly in check. Like other New England boys he had shouldered a fowling-piece from the entry to his teens, and in mature years he sometimes found himself 'seeking some kind of venison which he might devour, and no morsel could have been too savage'; yet he discovered that he could not even indulge in his favourite pastime of angling 'without failing a little in self-respect.'

It would be impossible to unravel and enumerate one by one the bundle of impulses that drove Thoreau to Walden in the year 1845, in the twenty-eighth year of his age. For nearly a decade Fourier's idea of the Phalanstery had been in the air, and as early as 1841 Thoreau had conceived a modification of it. He would build a hut by the shore of Walden, and as he watched the seasons pacing in their ceaseless minuet would study Nature and make a theory of the universe and quiet his own strivings and school himself to live as still and imperturbable as field and woodside and forest. How he borrowed an axe and reared himself a dwelling, how he delved and ploughed and fished he has himself told better than any other. For us it only remains to disentangle the valuable from the worthless of the results.

Many biographers and apologists have protested because critics such as Mr. Louis Stevenson and Mr. Lowell assert Thoreau to have been an idler; but his life was a protest against 'the modern heresy of work.' Nothing is more typical of his doctrine than the following passage from Walden : 'Men say that a stitch in time saves nine and so they take a thousand stitches to-day to save nine to-morrow. As for *work* we haven't any of any consequence.' How to extract the maximum of enjoyment out of life with a minimum of

exertion is not a problem that would have suggested
itself to one who believed in a mission to toil. Yet
here we seem to see the very rock on which his life
made shipwreck, for never was there a less qualified
evangelist of idleness. The doctrine was grafted on
one of those ceaselessly active, pushing, energetic
natures that live as though there were an eternity to
rest in. Even in his woodland hut he could not
constrain himself with all his force of will into the rich
dreamy indolence from which Jefferies could hardly
emerge. Look at the pictures he has made of himself :
is there one of sloth? You see him up before the
summer sunrise and plunging into the pond while
flowers still wet with dew cast their long morning
shadows on the water; then home to set his furniture
out on the grass, 'my three-legged table, from which I
did not remove the books and pens and ink, standing
amidst the pines and hickories' ; while he scrubbed and
swept and dusted till the cleanliness of the cottage
would have done credit to the most orderly housewife
of Boston. Next behold him cooking his simple
breakfast, and then as early as the farm-labourer out on
the bean-field, where ' my hoe tinkled against the stones,'
and 'that music echoed to the woods and the sky.' If
he had an interlude from labour it deserves chronicling.
'Sometimes in a summer morning,' he says, 'having
taken my accustomed bath, I sat in my sunny doorway
from sunrise till noon, rapt in a reverie, amidst the
pines and hickories and sumachs, in undisturbed
solitude and stillness, while the birds sang around, or
flitted noiselessly through the house, until by the sun
falling in at my west window, or the noise of some
traveller's wagon on the distant highway, I was

reminded of the lapse of time.' But did Thoreau know from actual experience what it is 'to dream and dream like yonder amber light'? If he did, the creations of his imagination died as they were born. One might infer from his writing that during those forenoons he was rapt in fruitless attempts to simplify his compound fraction, and that he was no more an idler than the chess-player, who seemingly inactive wastes the lamp-light over a problem. The care and regularity with which his diaries were kept, the rapidity with which his writing was done, and the peculiar fitness of his epithets afford plain proof that on the lake or in the forest he was continually on the watch for fact, continu-ally searching for expression. If he ever attained to anything like real idleness it was in the moonlit hours when he walked fluting on the pond's sandy shore. You cannot imagine him, as you may Jefferies, wholly abandoned to the dreamless and forgetful sensuousness of living, the joy of receiving on the senses without thought or reflection—impassively, as we may imagine a flower taking the kisses of the wind—the impressions of sunlight and colour and sound. His physique was a contradiction of his creed. The innate idler is of a soft and corpulent habit of body, his eye restful and languid, his muscles unstrung, his motions easy and slow, his speech trickling, and ever in search of an excuse to stop. He rests i' the sun like one who has eaten of lotos, and allows the warmth and the breeze, the greenery of Nature and her music to build picture and procession, to erect groves and to trace rivers and to people this land of fancy with beauteous nymph and naiad. But it all comes as involuntarily, as unbidden, as independent of exertion as a dream.

F

Thoreau was the reverse of that. His originally poor figure was hardened by exertion till the muscles were like whipcord, and his pedestrian achievements were those of an athlete. No true exponent of sloth could have become so lean, sinewy, and active; a paragon to run and swim and leap. His clear voice and sharp eager glance might have belonged to a successful shop-keeper, in contrast to those of Coleridge, for example, that inborn sluggard. In deepest repose you still fancy that his axe is lying at the foot of some tree, real or metaphorical, and that in a moment he may rise and smite. For the man at root is a bustling, energetic Yankee, hopelessly paralysed by a (to him) unnatural doctrine of idleness that itself is a twisted and tortured form of Emersonian Transcendentalism. His life was a violent contradiction to his theories. There is no work worth doing he said, and all the time toiled like a slave. On one important point only did he differ from others, and this was in regard to payment. The world seemed to say to him, ' I do not think it of importance to have an inspector of snow-storms and rain-storms, a surveyor of forest paths, a man to water the red huckleberry, the sand cherry, and the nettle-tree, and I will not pay you much for it. If, however, you will forswear this work and take up a common craft; if you will go into trade, or become a tutor or school-master, a clerk or a hack-writer, you shall have the wherewith to buy for yourself comfort and luxuries.' Now Thoreau did not highly esteem this offer. It made him turn round and ask rather sharply what the comforts were that had been offered for a lifetime of uncongenial drudgery. The answer was that he would have two coverlets where one was sufficient, two beds of which one must be tenantless, a carriage when he preferred to walk, table delicacies ill-suited to his digestion, treasure for moth and rust. He saw his fellow-men unhesitatingly close with the offer. In countless myriads they were industriously making their thousand stitches to-day to save nine to-morrow. For the sake of houses and lands never to be enjoyed by them, for wealth utterly useless, for advancement and position pregnant with new trouble and discontent, men forsook the sky and the hillside, the forest glade and the river bank for choking nauseous streets, for an unending torment of figures, a ceaseless addition and subtraction and multiplication of money columns. They have been doing so for centuries with hardly an independent voice ever raised to question the general belief. Thoreau refused to follow the multitude, and with bold hardihood declined the drudgery and the wages. He was one of the few with sufficient courage to deliberately weigh the proposal. A crust of bread and a cup of water in the silence and amid the pines of Walden were more to him than seven courses in a city restaurant. The rewards of ambition were in his eyes only so many evil apparitions. It was a question of temperament. 'I wanted to live deep and suck out all the marrow of life,' but so do others who load themselves with cares and perplexities that they may with the burden still upon them take hurried gulps of pleasure. A more passionate and sensuous man than he would have scouted the idea of 'the essential facts of life' having been fronted in seclusion from love and strife, in stoical abstinence and inexperience.

Yet Thoreau was a fastidious though simple epicure. He loved to pluck his berries as they hung fresh and cool in the glade, and feel as he ate them the sharp sweet tang of the forest, spices and seasonings deliberately rejected. 'If I strike out,' he argued, 'artificial appetites and superfluous desires and un- necessary wants so may I also gain by ridding myself of the trouble of supplying them.' The morning sun might rise without signalling him to labour, the evening shadows close in and bring no care. If we could fancy Rip Van Winkle dead to all else yet alive to sunshine and wind, the music of Nature and the colour of flowers, that would nearly be the ideal of Thoreau. But there was still a serpent in his Eden. He deafened himself to the trumpet blast that, like the peasant's horn at yoking time, calls most of us to daily action, yet he was not satisfied. Something made him ask continually what life is and what it teaches, and by no complacent dogmatism could he brush the queries aside. He was distracted even from the study of Nature by a doubting, questioning, criticising, philosophy.

That constitutes the main point of difference between him and Jefferies. If the latter had anything artificial in his nature, it was his desire born of need and ambi- tion to rush into the human throng. Nevertheless, he lived the very life Thoreau aspired to. In the heart of crowded England, close to London, unschooled, trained amid the jabber of modern journalism, he could be nothing but solitary. When he describes wild things and cornfields and pasture, his reader feels that the world might be destitute of human inhabitants. Let him only be in the open air, under the blue sky and the drifting clouds, the sunshine falling on the brook, the wind blowing from the downs, and for him and for us there is nothing but the present moment, neither past nor present, nor questions of the day, nor hopes, nor griefs, nor sorrows, only a cluster of senses fed and ministered to by the elements. The fitful fever of modern life was not upon him. As patiently and tranquilly as any cloistered monkish carver, or school-master of the Middle Ages, he amasses his wonderful details, and connects them with nothing save his own ardent love of each. It is hardly possible for the reader to believe that this perfect and beautiful fresh-ness emanates from a young man of the jaded, fretful, striving nineteenth century. So also in the facts of his life. It was unnecessary for him in his maturity to build a hut or rent a cottage on the Wiltshire Downs to observe or to think; wherever his house was, Goring or Surbiton or anywhere else, he still to the end of his days lived in solitude at Coate. And yet it was by no conscious effort of the imagination. Let him take pen in hand, and to whatever point of the compass he tries to direct his thoughts, the Swindon copses and spinnies, the meadows, the follies on the hilltop get themselves painted on his paper. He was the most perfectly un-sophisticated and natural man of his time.

To all this Thoreau offers an exact and striking con-trast. He never was out of America, and with the exception of one or two short periods, the whole of his life was spent in and about Concord, yet his reflections might have come from Fleet Street. His railings against the world, his protests against luxury and com-petition, his fierce condemnation of the aims and labour of his fellow-men are more suggestive of a disappointed cit than of an ingenuous wild man of the woods. At college and at the feet of Emerson he had imbibed a second-hand and discoloured Carlylean philosophy, the effect of which was to spoil him for his obvious life-work. Without it he might have developed into a great naturalist, one to inform that science with new life, and from that pursuit he would assuredly have sucked more pleasure than from hoeing beans and surveying wood lots. The world is not after all so stupid as to refuse a livelihood for a service that his journals prove Thoreau to have been eminently capable of rendering. There was an element of weakness in his character, however, that led him to curb and hamper his inclinations in small things and in great.

Just as he was a born hunter who forswore the gun, scrupled at the angle, and refused to eat flesh, so also he was a most companionable man who chose an artificial solitude. If he made an excursion, he was as careful to look out for a fellow-traveller, as is the ordinary pedestrian tourist. He was 'a man of good fellowship' who loved a 'dish of gossip,' and one who never could stay long away from his fellows; and it was not long before he wearied of the Walden loneliness. Though love of out-of-door life was the predominant feature of his character, he must needs sandwich his descriptions with preaching and moralisation about a world of which he was ignorant. When the editors of the future approach their inevitable duty of separating the dead from the living in the swiftly accumulating literature of our time, the works of Thoreau will be the easiest to deal with; all they require is for every passage with a precept, a teaching or a doctrine to be ruthlessly excised, and the remainder will be his lasting and valuable contribution.

Students of extraordinary phenomena, those who

have described the avalanche, the earthquake, and the volcano, great battles by sea and land, plague, famine, and tempest, untrodden mountain tops, unfurrowed seas, and lands virgin to the explorer, may well ask in wonder the secret of that charm by which Thoreau pins the interest of his hearer to things the most trivial and homely—a warfare of emmets, the helve of a lost axe waving at the bottom of a pond, the musical thrum of telegraph wires, an owl's hooting, or a cockerel's cry. When a Pasteur deals with bacteria infinitely smaller, or a Darwin examines the infinitesimal grains of sand borne hither on a migrant's feet, a further interest of science is reflected on the description. It is not so with Thoreau; he aims neither at an exhaustive and orderly examination nor at discovery. He was a correspondent and helper of Agassiz, but not himself a toiler in the field of formal natural history, and he declined to write for the Boston Society, because he could not properly detach the mere external record of observation from the inner associations with which such facts were connected in his mind. To have laboured for the increase of positive knowledge would have been heresy to his doctrine of idleness. No one reads *Walden* for information.

Still less is the interest traceable to theology. The Christian, who sees in Nature the handiwork of Him whose design includes every twittering sparrow and unnoticed weed, dare be indifferent to no minutest detail of the system that reveals to him a Creator's omnipotence. The rugged thornbush and the revolving planet, the tiny glow-worm and the beasts of the forest, the humming-bird and the red lily, whose chalice holds its food, 'these are thy works, Almighty Father.' Of

that Thoreau was by no means certain; for it had been
'somewhat hastily concluded,' he said, 'that it is the
chief end of man to glorify God.' Nor did he adopt
the lofty Transcendental creed that the universe is 'the
vesture of God.' Indeed, opinions such as these formed
the unanswered puzzle of his life. He was a mystic, a
theist, a believer in the immortality of the soul, but
hesitatingly and doubtfully. Even the pantheism of
which so much has been said inspires little of his
writing. Nor do the 'inner associations' of which he
says so much account for our interest.

Were a man's analysis of his own impulses trustworthy, the following passage would set forth Thoreau's
radical ideas :—

> 'Then idle time ran gadding by
> And left me with eternity alone ;
> I hear beyond the range of sound,
> I see beyond the range of sight.

I see, smell, taste, hear, feel that everlasting something to which we are allied, at once our maker, our
abode, our destiny, our very selves; the one historic
truth, the most remarkable fact which can become the
distinct and uninvited subject of our thought, the
actual glory of the universe, the only fact which a
human being cannot avoid recognising.' What that
something precisely is was the x of his simplified
fraction. Whatever it was, it inspired him with a
belief closely akin to Eastern fatalism and that Christian resignation expressed in confidence that the ways
of Providence are just. 'Nothing can rightly compel a
simple and brave man to a vulgar sadness,' he says, as
if through devious ways the unseen force were driving
us on to a great end. 'The Lord gave, and the Lord

hath taken away; blessed be the name of the Lord,' cried the just man of Uz in the same spirit.

Every abiding religion and enduring philosophy and truthful thought rests on the cardinal principle from which Thoreau's optimism and the Christian faith have come. 'Dust we are,' says Darwin as well as Moses, and, as Carlyle had it, 'the natural and supernatural are one.' Whether it be that we, as creations of Divine power are individually immortal, or but strangely carved conduits built by imprisoned force as avenues for its own escape, we still are but portions of the illimitable power that governs the universe. Modern creeds and ancient mythologies are but expressions in complicated terms of a simple truth that, whatever be its formulation, is the belief of every man and every age. Yet Nature is a mother of warring children, and it was easier for the hermit to hold an abstract doctrine than for others to practise it. He tells how he used to feel his way in the dead of night through the pitch-dark Walden forest while his mind was full of merry thoughts. And again, 'There was never yet such a storm but it was Æolian music to a healthy and innocent ear.' One thinks of seamen in a roaring tempest, bleared and chilled by the icy waves and battling for life—and wonders. When the wild billows have settled to a slow spasmodic heaving, and the shore is strewn with dead bodies as well as sea-weed and wreckage, is not the onlooker who thinks of the widows and fatherless filled with a compassion closely akin to 'vulgar sadness'?

It has been said that Thoreau was a man without pity or tenderness, and his essay on winter animals goes far to prove the assertion. From no other season does he seem to have extracted a deeper enjoyment. The fox howls in an agony of hunger, and he criticises the notes as calmly as a *connoisseur* in a concert room. So with the red squirrels that came to his roof, the lean and bony hare, the starved rabbits, the wrangling jays and chicadees; there is never a word of the suffering brought by the snow, but a keen appreciation of motion and colour and attitude. Old age he did not at all respect, and he is never struck by the pathos of seeing everything gradually lose its capacity for fruitfulness and pleasure. Years carry decay to the forest trees and stiffen the wild deer's sinews and draw the fangs from fox and serpent, but they suggest no sorrow to him. It was not so with Jefferies, who never touches on such themes except in terms of piercing and passionate regret. And his was the richer and deeper temperament. From certain high altitudes of philosophy it is possible to look down with a serenity on struggle and suffering that must be preliminary to some beneficent result, but that was not Thoreau's position. 'He jests at scars who never felt a wound,' and this placid non-combatant makes light of a strife from which he lived apart. If eternity be more than a name for oblivion, Time's 'roaring loom' is not idle; if it be only that the inmost truth of most things is sorrow.

Thoreau's Transcendentalism was a creed modified to suit an individuality, and is as worthy of study as that of Carlyle or Emerson or Goethe, but here it is interesting only so far as it affected his study of Nature. Habitually he spoke slightingly of art, and a certain jerky changeableness of style, a lack of capacity to build and arrange his ideas, to produce completed forms, show that the opinion was a natural outcome of temperament. Yet the red heat of genius is in his descriptions. The man is paramount in the excellence of his scenes. When he attempts poetry it is obvious enough that he has no command of the fiery material of that craft, the melting tenderness, the burning passion, the infinite regret that Homer and Shakespeare and Burns present to us in magical and immortal chalices. But on the other hand that high ecstasy and enthusiasm, 'the vision and faculty divine,' that the romantic incidents of life excite in others was aroused in him by the simple exercise of common physical attributes.

There is something Transcendental in all enduring literature, and especially in that belonging to the Saxon race. Till the primal secrets are disclosed and the sepulchre of hope is sealed, love will not be wholly lust, but mystical and transcendent; in friendship, in valour, in hatred, in joy and labour and sorrow there will still remain the same 'inner something' that Thoreau discerned in every flower and pebble. In primitive times, when men as it were surveyed the past and present from the first landing-place, ignorance and fear and superstition lent the darkness horror, but now when we have as it seems traversed the whole island of knowledge and come in view of the further shore we still are confronted with the inexplicable.

Thoreau's Mysticism, though born out of due time, is purely Darwinian. In that Walden wood he stands as the most wonderful and sensitive register of phenomena, finer and more exact than any cunningly devised measure. He is vision and hearing, touch, smelling, and taste incarnate. Not only so, but he knows how to preserve the flashing forest colours in unfading light, to write down the wind's music in a score that all may

read, to glean and garner every sensuous impression.
Physical science tells us that the sun's rays, the beating
pulses of sound, and other natural forces or forms of
force have built up man—'the beauty of the world, the
paragon of animals'; they have hollowed out his ear
and taught his eye to see and his mouth to speak. The
experiment of Thoreau carries us face to face with a
mystery beyond that. He cleansed his mind of every
accepted cosmogony and idle superstition, he brushed
aside all common aims and ambitions, he conformed to
hygienic law and subdued his unclean sensual lusts.
'If the day and the night are such,' he says, 'that you
greet them with joy, and life emits a fragrance like
flowers and sweet-scented herbs, is more elastic, more
starry, more immortal—that is your success.' But if
you reduce yourself to utter stillness, if you creep out
of the world's strife and let Nature sing to you and
show her picture-book, does that wending of force
through the delicate channels it has formed constitute
life ?

Thoreau's answer was a vigorous and decided nega-
tive. 'However intense my experience,' he says, 'I am
conscious of the presence and criticism of a part of me
which, as it were, is not a part of me, but spectator,
sharing no experience but taking note of it; and that is
no more I than it is you.' And this it is that makes
of the wild man's life a perpetual wonder. When the
sunny lake smiles is it conscious of its joy ? The
tussocky grass on the hill-side and the grey boulder
reclining on it are as mysterious as the Alps. Why
should every wretched wild-fowl guard its existence as
warily and jealously as a pure virgin her honour ? At
one moment the sight, nay, the mere fragrance of a

natural object that usually goes unreguarded comes clear and bright and vivid as a revelation, establishing as it were the kinship, almost the identity, of man with the animate and inanimate matter around him. At another, mind soaring away beyond star and planet, gifted with foresight and memory and imagination, informed with daring hope and fair dream, claims a high and intransient sovereignty over everything else.

And so it happens that Thoreau's long toil at his algebraical fraction left it still unsimplified. He could not at the end give any more explicit information about life than was already in our possession, and he did not commend his philosophy of idleness so engagingly that others are inclined to adopt it. But for the courage with which, setting aside the traditions formed by ages and generations of men, he faced the eternal problem boldly and only with the forces of his own understanding, he deserves our gratitude. The spirit of his dream could come upon the great army of 'men the workers only as enervation and paralysis, but it is good that life should be studied from every stand-point, especially from the heights and hollows unseen by the great body of pilgrims that sweats along the common and dusty highway. A Petrarch has his use as well as a Carlyle, a Herbert as well as a Villon; and whatever other merit may be denied Thoreau it must be granted that his philosophy has the peculiar freshness that comes from studying life and Nature by no conventional and traditional methods, but as they naturally present themselves to an individual gifted with independence.

IV

THE ROMANCE OF LIFE

(SCOTT)

THAT student of Nature must be indeed unreflective who has not mused on the fact that dismayed the author of *In Memoriam*, how 'red in tooth and claw,' 'of fifty seeds she often brings but one to bear.' Amid the tinted withering leaves of autumn there is nothing more striking than her profuse preparation for spring. The gentlest breeze on the sunniest day gathers and sows again for a harvest never to ripen. Dainty wild flowers are shedding their flossy seedlets in myriads, ruddy hedgerow and thicket hold out promise of new wildernesses, and flocks of young birds seem threatento overrun the earth. On a single clump of oaks there are acorns enow to afforest a county; yet, of many successive crops, it is doubtful if a solitary nut will be allowed to grow. Were you able to sit invisible on the dry trunk in the middle of the little wood you would see how the great store is gradually diminished. Tattered and laughing children from the hamlet carry off bagfuls after every strong gale, the wood pigeon with a clatter of wings, the jay with a discordant cry come for their share, and the domestic pig fattens on what he routs up from the mouldering leafage. Some are blown into the stagnant, festering ditch, a few are dropped on the road and bruised by passing cartwheels. The only survivor has very likely been carried off by a bird and accidentally laid on congenial soil.

It is the same with men. A million poets are born and all, save perhaps one, are devoured by their common mother. We know sound acorns when we see them; the nurseryman who desires it will make a bushel of them sprout; but on the foreheads of children there is no mark to say which has and which has not the capacity of greatness. Mute, inglorious Miltons and village Hampdens live ineffectually and die unrecognised. Some have been deflected from their course by riches, some by poverty, some lured to a bootless quest of learning, some chained to earth by ignorance. But in any case till power has flowered into achievement, our limited senses tell us little of it. Yet the study of biography teaches nothing with more absolute certainty than that greatness is the offspring of ability and environment; as the young oak of our illustration owed its existence no less to the bird's unconscious interference than to the acorn it sprang from.

Of the truth of this doctrine it were impossible to cite a more brilliant proof than the life of Sir Walter Scott. Somersby did not do so much for Tennyson, or Coate for Jefferies, as the Borderland did for the child born to be its minstrel. The blood of many fiery chieftains, of Beardie and Auld Wat of Harden, of John the Lamiter and William Boltfoot, flowed in his veins and in his peaceable annals is abundant testimony that had he lived in earlier and more stirring times he would have been no cleric like Gawin Douglas, but a trooper as bold as his own William of Deloraine, a lover as

romantic as any hero of the *Waverley Novels*; while the
King Richard of his fancy had no keener relish for
venison pasty, or Gentle King Jamie a readier hearing
for wit. In aims and character, in conduct, ambition, and
the nature of his enjoyment he furnishes a more striking
contrast to Thoreau than is done even by the great
prophet of labour himself. Yet as, beyond question or
cavil or doubt, he is the most popular writer, not only
of his generation, but of his century, one whose fame,
instead of flashing like a meteor then dwindling into
obscurity, shines on with growing and unclouded
splendour, it may be assumed that his unconscious, or
at any rate unobtruded philosophy comes nearer the
truth than that of others who have formulated their
wisdom. It is of considerable interest therefore to note
the process by means of which this oak was fostered
into the monarchy of the forest.

Scott was as fortunate in his immediate parents as
in his ancestry. While his father was a grave and
kindly, upright and successful man such as any son
might be proud of, his mother acted nurse to the future
poet and novelist as well as to her baby. Her humour
and her narrative skill, her lore in legend and tradition,
her love of reading and verse afforded the stimulation
her child's task needed. And yet, if deep associations
and abiding memories constitute home, that of Scott's
boyhood was not in the house where he was born at
the head of the College Wynd in Edinburgh, but
at Sandyknowe in Berwickshire, whence his father
had come. There, as he has told us himself in the
most tender of his poems, he garnered impressions that
endured for a lifetime. Nor was the helplessness to
which he was reduced wholly a misfortune. A spirited

and vivacious boy intent on active amusement hears but scarcely heeds the talk of his elders; he would sooner romp among the hayricks or roam the burnside and the brae than listen to the most thrilling stories. The wakening fancy was in this case, however, the substitute for activity; for the boy was fettered by disease, and it was to his and our gain that the amusement provided to wile away the tedium of the hours was peculiarly adapted to feed and develop his genius. Sandy Ormistone the aged hind, who on fine mornings bore him shoulder high to 'the green hill and clear blue heaven,' was in his talk as innocent of ulterior intention as the migrating bird that amid the sand clinging to its feet brings a new seed to a continent. But he taught his little charge the lore he knew; showed where the broad blue flank of Cheviot rose in the horizon; pointed to Smailholm's shattered tower, and ransacked his memory for tales of the bold marauders who rode over and ravaged adjacent Northumberland, and made the old halls ring with revelry till

> ' Methought, grim features, seam'd with scars,
> Glared through the window's rusty bars.'

Indoors the evening diversion was to listen to more of these legends. 'My grandmother,' says Scott in the autobiographical fragment prefixed to Lockhart's *Life*, 'in whose youth the old Border depredations were matter of recent tradition, used to tell me many a tale of Watt of Harden, Wight Willie of Aikwood, Jamie Telfer of the fair Dodhead, and other heroes—merrymen all of the persuasion and calling of Robin Hood and Little John. A more recent hero, but not of less note, was the celebrated Deil of Littledean, whom she well remembered, as he had married her brother's sister.' Besides

this delightful old lady, there was an occasional visitor
who had seen relatives of the family executed at
Carlisle for being out in the '45, thus lending vividness
to the songs and tales of the Jacobites; and a kind and
affectionate aunt who read to him from *Automathes*
and Allan Ramsay. Already therefore the small
lamiter's mind was full to overflowing

> 'Of lovers' slights, of ladies' charms,
> Of witches' spells, of warriors' arms.'

They were all he had to think about, and when the
farm-house talk turned to crops and cattle, to eggs and
butter, and markets and fairs, it is easy to picture the
winter hearth :—

> 'While stretch'd at length upon the floor
> Again I fought each combat o'er,
> Pebbles and shells in order laid,
> The mimic ranks of war display'd :
> And onward still the Scottish lion bore,
> And still the scatter'd Southron fled before.'

All the elements of that Scottish life he afterwards
pourtrayed so incomparably were present at Sandyknowe,
where Scott with one or two short breaks lived till he
was eight. There were the lessons read at night from
the big ha' Bible; the typical minister, acrid, yet good-
hearted, emaciated, tall, 'his legs cased in clasped
gambadoes'; there were the disputations on doctrine
typical of the country; and bickerings over march and
fence, flock and herd, in which his grandfather used
commonly to act as arbiter. In naked, rudely piled
cliffs and barren moors there was a taste of Scotland's
sternly characteristic scenery. But beyond all else the
memory of stirring events still lay warm on keep
and tower. To this day you may hear rosy lasses at

the ewe-buchts singing as they milk of the Broom o'
Cowdenknowes, or the Death of Lord Ronald, and
some perhaps are grandchildren of the laughing girls
who sang the same tunes to the lame child whom they
carried about the crags on their backs. The rugged and
independent, yet tender and kindly Border peasant is
chokeful of superstition, and as Scott's own grandfather
tried to cure the bad leg by a magical charm, it is easy
to see that here the young wizard laid the foundation of
that love of gramarye that was developed in his later
life. And all these things grew pleasanter in the lad's
memory because they were associated with the happiness of returning health. The amateur doctors found
that for him from morning till night to roll about on
the green sward amid sheep, every one of which he
knew by headmark, was a spell of more efficacy than
the other of laying him on the floor wrapped in a dead
fleece. By degrees he recovered the use of his
shrivelled limb to the extent of being able to walk and
even run.

To us who review his life it seems as though every
little event marshalled Scott the way that he was going,
and that he was fortunate in coming into contact with
minds of close affinity to his own. The attention paid
him at Bath by the venerable author of *Douglas*; his
intimacy at Prestonpans with the military veteran
Dalgetty, who had been through the German wars, and
entertained him with stirring reminiscences of them;
and his early friendship with his aunt's forlorn lover,
George Constable, the prototype in a way of Jonathan
Oldbuck; the kindly interest taken in him by Dr.
Blacklock, who introduced him to Ossian and Spenser,
were all forces tending to deepen and expand his know-

ledge of Scottish life and literature. At the High School of Edinburgh, Scott showed how impossible it is for a boy of lively imagination to concentrate his mind on the acquisition of knowledge. People sometimes ask in amazement what becomes of those who ravish school and university of their honours, and talk as though it would have been but natural had the Prime Ministers of England all been senior wranglers. But the very forces that enable a man to push along the narrow and difficult groove that leads to academic distinctions are adverse to the roaming speculativeness that is the basis of originality. It was a regret of Scott's life that he never became an accurate and finished scholar ; but how could he have done so ? He confesses to the indolence that, though he knew it not, is inseparable from genius like his, and, tremendous toiler as he was, he lamented two years before his death (and frequently before that) a 'strange desire to leave a prescribed task and set about something else.' The charms of general reading were in his case stronger than those of grammar or etymology, and even *it* was not accomplished in a way to pass examinations, for as often as not he began in the middle or end of a book and prided himself on a knack of extracting the essence of the interest. Without being a dunce in school he fell short of attaining distinction, and the highest eulogy he earned was that of Dr. Adam, the rector, that although many of the pupils knew the Latin better, ' Gualterus Scott was behind few in following and enjoying the author's meaning.' The boy was not qualifying to be a pedant, but had there been any examination to test his mastery of ideas none would have been in front of him.

It is comparatively seldom, however, that the training
of any remarkable man receives its main impulse from
school or college. When Scott, unable by reason of
his lameness to share in rough sports, was in a corner
of the playground taxing his ingenuity and imagination so to invent and relate stories as to be sure of an
audience, he was exercising his intellect more fruit-
fully than was possible in any class. And a glance at
the occupations of his hours of leisure shows that the
knowledge he stood most in need of was pouring in
from many channels. The Borders remained to him a
land of enchantment, and their rude traditionary
minstrelsy, of which he learned more and more during
repeated holiday visits, began as he grew older to dis-
close a world of romance wherein men in buff jerkin
armed with crossbow and poleaxe performed unheard-of
feats of valour for the sake of golden-haired May or
Flower; and with every new peep his appetite grew
more insatiable. Even in infancy he had begun to
collect old ballads, of which his own mother and the
mother of his playmate, John Irving, had a large stock
in memory. Before he was ten years old he had bound
up several volumes of these, as well as penny chap-
books and things of a like nature. He has told us himself how the pursuit developed into a passion. 'I
fastened like a tiger,' he says, 'upon every collection of
old songs or romances which chance threw in my way.'
His first perusal of Percy's *Reliques* 'was beneath a
huge platanus-tree, in the ruins of what had been in-
tended for an old-fashioned arbour in the garden. . . .
The summer-day sped onward so fast, that notwith-
standing the sharp appetite of thirteen, I forgot the
hour of dinner, was sought for with anxiety,

and was still found entranced in my intellectual ban-
quet.' In view of these facts it seems ridiculous that
Carlyle, in the least creditable of his essays, should have
derived the origin of the minstrelsy from the *Götz von
Berlichingen* of Goethe. On the contrary this taste of
Scott's was an easy and natural outcome of his circumstances. His interest was kindled by the tales and
legends told during his periodical visits, and whetted
by the feeling that in many a wild raid and foray the
forefathers of whom he was proud had borne a leading
part.

But indeed the dullest and most indifferent boy, sent
as he was to school at Kelso after the close of his High
School curriculum, could hardly have avoided the stimulation of his curiosity by the surroundings of that
beautiful little town, and in Scott's case the intellect
was kept bright and active; not only by Lancelot Whale
the clever schoolmaster, but by the talk of his intelligent and affectionate aunt. We love the scenery where
we have been happy, and song or story was hardly
needed to enchant him with the broad Tweed and silver
Teviot. There were close at hand he tells us 'the ruins
of an ancient abbey, the more distant vestiges of
Roxburgh Castle, the modern mansion of Fleurs.'
And even then, I fancy, his thoughts must often have
strayed some score of miles southward to a district
across the march, where, in the wildest battle ever
fought on the Borders, 'the flowers of the forest were a'
wede away.' Flodden, dark with its crown of oaks, the
sullen and deadly Till washing its distant base, the lone
and sleeping Cheviots behind them, with all the old
or ruined fortresses renowned in Northumbrian legends,
Etal and Ford, Norham's castled steep and Twizel's

exquisite dell and ancient bridge, Wark and Coupland and Chillingham, and a hundred others were already familiar by repute, and needed but a visit to shape themselves into the material of *Marmion*.

Scott tells us that at Kelso he first began to take delight in picturesque scenery, and hardly anything could be franker than his analysis of the pleasure. Of the naturalist's love of detail, or of minute fact, which Thoreau and Jefferies possessed to such a remarkable degree he had literally none. Nor is there in his poetry anything analogous to the elaborately painted flowers, laburnum, and tulip, and marigold, that occur in the verse of Tennyson like illuminations in a mediæval manuscript. And to pursue our negation further, he never felt the mysterious communion with Nature that is born of deepest solitude. It never occurred to his simple and natural mind that anything was to be gained by forcibly and artificially divorcing himself from the human interests that gradually twine around life. In one sense he hardly ever was alone; for his apparently solitary hours, when his restless unpausing pen travelled incessantly across and across the page of foolscap: or those others when, still as its own statuary, he sat amid the ruins of Melrose Abbey, or blent with the land-scape looked to the Eildons or listened to Tweed ever raving on its bed of gravel, were enlivened with a troop of familiars whose lives he both ordered and lived. When his imagination gave him holiday, his brain still teemed with projects of business or pleasure, that nothing either in his temperament or in his training ever taught him to disdain. Thus his works bear no testimony to any of the deep questioning of Nature that made Shakespeare at times view the world as 'the baseless fabric of a vision,' or 'glimpses of the moon'; and that appears to have been Carlyle's warranty for saying that his love of Nature was 'not more genuine than has dwelt in hundreds of men named minor poets.' Later criticism also in agreeing to call him eulogistically 'a master of the commonplace' admits without bewailing the same lack of fiery ardour.

Scott's biography is the true key to his art, and attracts us for reasons the exact opposite of those that lend fascination to the records of him who has brooded over the mystery of existence. He was not the chemist who analyses the contents of the cup of life, but he who quaffs them to the lees. There is no saner and more joyous youth than his told of in the annals of English literature; though, were our knowledge more complete, it would probably be found that Shakespeare's equalled it in full-blooded gaiety. Look how warm with happiness and content are the successive pictures of his career! Melancholy broods over the history of other men of letters. An unhappy hunger of fame within and huge obstacles without, labour and pain in the acquisition of knowledge, discouragement, privation, and misery have long been the concomitants of literary genius. But like some barque that is borne slowly into haven on the tide, Scott without preliminary struggle or suffering drifted surely and steadily into the authorship, for which his early years had been a prolonged preparation.

The history of his adolescence is as charming as that of any ideal hero in a story book, and the shrewd remark of Mr. Shortreed about the famous raids into Liddesdale might be applied to all the first thirty years of his life: 'He was makin' himsell a' the time; but he didna

ken maybe what he was about till years had passed ; at
first he thought o' little, I dare say, but the queerness
and the fun.' Education, alike at College and High
School, was but a light and easy pastime diversified by
visits to Borderland, each of which deepened and
fixed the early impressions produced by that romantic
district. He was a loyal law apprentice to his father,
but the only record of toilsome labour in that capacity
is the tale of his copying one hundred and twenty folios
at a sitting for the sake of pocket-money wherewith to
defray the expenses of theatre and library. And even
this position provided him with materials for his craft,
for at his fifteenth year, just when he was beginning to
take a keen enjoyment of natural scenery, his father's
business led him to the very heart of the Highlands, in
company with a Highland sergeant full to overflowing
with tales of Rob Roy : so that it became easy to fancy
the outlaw's skiff once more on Loch Ard, or imagine
Ellen skimming the blue waters of Loch Katrine, to fill
the clachans with English troopers and the glens with
caterans, while the majesty of the great Bens, towering
in purple and seamed with white lines of cascade, and
the craggy difficult passes, bordered with green pine
and tremulous birch, were well calculated to enhance
the boy's eager and splendid vision of the past.

As he grew older and his constitution became
strengthened till he could take a thirty mile tramp and
not feel weary, love of Nature in the form of admiration
for scenery led him at every opportunity to make
similar excursions on horse or foot. The character of
his mind, however, is nowhere better exemplified than
in this, that the associations connected with a place
transcended its form and colour in interest. When you

read Jefferies at his best man seems to have either
faded from the landscape or be reduced in significance
till he stands on a level with roaming wild beast or
restless bird. But with Scott the ancient harp of
Caledon is greater than the witch-elm on which it hangs ;
the river does not murmur on imperturbably indifferent
to what succeeding races float their shallops on its wave
or lap its waters, but murmurs dirges round the poet's
grave. He prizes the glen for its legend and the
mountain cave for its goblin. The picturesque in action
was more to him than the picturesque in scenery.
'Show me an old castle or field of battle,' he says, 'and
I was at home at once, filled it with its combatants in
their proper costume, and overwhelmed my hearers with
the enthusiasm of my descriptions.' In this there was
beyond question some of the Border clansman's love of
arms and strife. After many generations had prided
themselves on sword and fortress, it would have been
strange indeed had their descendant whose lot fell in
more peaceable times not still retained a taste for the
ancient tools.

Deeper than that, however, was the fact that Scott
was more concerned with living than with looking on.
The falsest dream of any man of letters is that from
some fancied vantage-ground of art he may survey the
restless, throbbing world, and use this and the other
passion foreign to his own nature as material for a
picture of life. For the truth is quite otherwise. To
write an epic you must live an epic, and as you live so
will you write. Every man's life is a play ending with
a tragic fifth act : every man ere he dies has amassed
material for one original novel—were sayings of Carlyle's.
As you pilgrim from the cradle to the grave you are

the centre of a world that escorts you on the journey. It waxes and wanes, is alternately bright with sunshine and dark with clouds, yet still it preserves an individuality and a character derived from you, and it is composed, not only of the friends and foes who come and go and rise and fall like apparitions that flash from darkness or fly into it, but of kindred hosts quite as real, fashioned by imagination to people the elsewhere and the past.

Infinitely diverse as the people of this kingdom may appear, they are blended together and harmonised as perfectly as the cliff and river, hill and forest of a fair landscape seen in the red light of sunset. For every man supplies the colour of his own surroundings. The living form beside him is only what he perceives there, and no man fully knows his dearest friend; the dead are what he conceives them to have been; the creations of his imagination are built from experience; so that the *cosmos* derives tint and hue from personality. But the over-cultivated and self-conscious artist ignores altogether this primary and elementary principle. Though he may not have 'the imagination that shudders at the hell of Dante,' he has learned from books that it is an occasional attribute of humanity, and coldly piecing together his acquired knowledge makes an imitation of it. Still oftener he is devoid of humour, and yet knowing that it should be in literature, fashions a dismal appearance to make show with. The spurious counterfeit passes current for a time because it is shrewdly calculated to meet expectation; as a sportsman in the dusk will readily mistake a gray stone in the grass for a feeding hare if his field-craft tells him that his game should be there.

But the only serious charge ever brought against Scott as a man of letters amounts to no more than a complaint of his having been absolutely faithful to himself. In the whole course of his writings there is not in poetry or prose any passage so sad and bitter, yet so charged with deep and searching thought, as, for example, the Shakespearean lines beginning

> 'To-morrow, and to-morrow, and to-morrow,
> Creeps in this petty pace from day to day
> To the last syllable of recorded time :
> And all our yesterdays have lighted fools
> The way to dusty death.'

Those who compare his Field of Flodden with the battle-pieces of Homer also fail to take into account the greater depth of the early bard, whose loftiest strains are sung when from the edge of time he looks down into the dark abyss of death. A man must either be naturally of a brooding, meditative temperament, like, for instance, that of Sir Thomas Browne, or be the object of fate's hardest buffeting to realise the inexplicable riddles of life.

Scott accepted existence without asking what was its ultimate goal or real meaning. The picture of his early life up to the moment of his first great misfortune is one of sunny and perfect enjoyment. For his sympathy with almost every form of innocent life and pleasure was unbounded. If the kings and nobles of his imagination loved brawny men and noble steeds and strong hounds it was because these were the delights of their creator, who was as devoted to the chase as his own Fitz-James, a judge of horse-flesh as keen as any mediæval knight of his fancy. During the time in which he lived there was not a heartier sportsman in

all Scotland. 'Gilnockie, my man,' asked one of the
poet's colleagues of Scott's eldest boy, 'you cannot
surely help seeing that great people make more work
about your papa than they do about me or any other of
your *uncles*; what is it, do you suppose, that occasions
this?' The answer not only illustrates Scott's zeal for
the chase, but casts a beautiful light on the innate
modesty that kept him from making too much of his
literary successes in the home circle. 'It's commonly
him that sees the hare sitting.' Lockhart adds that in
jest he would frequently remark, in reference to his
quickness in catching 'the sparkle of the victim's eye,'
that 'whatever might be thought of him as a *maker*
he was an excellent *trouveur.*' His letters show that
during the tours made in the vigour of life sport divided
his pleasure with romance, and there are no pictures in
his biography more characteristic than those where he is
seen, the merriest of a merry band, shooting wild duck or
fishing for salmon, or riding to a coursing match on the
back of Sybil Grey. The scene in Abbotsford dining-
room on the evening of the annual hunt in its stirring life
and animation suggests the frolic of a fox-hunting squire
more than the relaxation of a literary worker—the
Ettrick Shepherd and his companions, each trolling out
his favourite song or telling his best story, the bowls of
hot punch emptied and filled and emptied again, and
the host, 'his face radiant, his laugh gay as childhood,
his chorus always ready.' And the manner in which he
trained his children to love horse and hound and to
disdain peril, so that even his daughter in tender years
was the companion of his mountain rides, and faced a
ford or swollen stream as unconcernedly as a moss-
trooper, shows what ideals lay nearest his heart. How

they endured to the very end of his life is proved by
the touching account of his last appearance on horse-
back to see a little sport with the greyhounds in the
company of his son, Major Scott, then on a visit to
Abbotsford. 'We witnessed a very pretty chase or two,'
says the biographer, 'on the opposite side of the water,
but his eye always followed the tall steed and his rider.
The father might well assure Lady Davy that "a hand-
somer fellow never put foot into stirrup." But when he
took a very high wall of loose stones, at which everybody
else *craned*, as easily and as elegantly as if it had been
a puddle in his stride, the old man's rapture was extreme.
"Look at him!" said he, "only look at him! now, isn't
he a fine fellow?"' If we remember withal how Scott
nursed and fostered the ancient and manly Border sports,
and how in the alarm of 1815 he raised and commanded
a troop of Border sharp-shooters, it is impossible
to view him as other than a mediæval marchman born
again into modern times. Had he lived two centuries
earlier he might without writing a line have been famous
as a hard-riding, deep-drinking, and valiant marauder.
And there is no example of romantic courage to be
found in the *Waverley Novels*, not that of Wilfred, nor
Lovel, nor Rob Roy, nor the gallant foster-brothers who
died for Hector, that is more than a painting of what
his own might have been.

There shines, however, on the whole body of his
romance a mellow radiance that came from something
else than the fighting and hunting instinct. In his
stories there is an element still more captivating than the
interest and excitement. Much of the finest imaginative
literature written since his time is the reverse of exhilarating—is almost distressing to read. An English taste

does not revel in Flaubert's masterly analysis of a provincial woman's progress to perdition, nor in M. Zola's studies of filth, nor in M. de Maupassant's brilliant delineation of a soldier-journalist's lasciviousness, nor yet in M. Daudet's clever expositions of debauched life, but these are only a degree or two more disagreeable than the performance of some of our own novelists. All the genius of Thackeray does not quite reconcile us to his endless pursuit of small meanness and paltry vice. It is not wholly agreeable to follow Dickens into the smoky scenery of London, and hear him tell of dens that are its festering sores, and the crimes that are an outcome of its feverish life. The eminent female novelists are still more depressing. *Robert Elsmere* has had a vogue comparable I suppose to that of *Ivanhoe*, but it is a sad book to read ; and whatever opinion may be held as to the literary *status* of George Eliot, there can be no question of the discouragement and gloom produced by her novels, working as they do almost invariably to sorrow by dull paths, irradiated here and there by much cold and bitter witticism and sparse little gleams of humour. But, united with the consummate ease of Scott's narrative and the breezy out-of-door wholesomeness that pervades it, there is a genial and kindly glow that belongs to the masters of the craft: that was one of the things Dumas could not reproduce from him. The same half-jesting, half-serious, laughing, earnestness that broadens to burlesque in Cervantes and bubbles in Le Sage and pervades Fielding twinkles in the eye of Scott. The smile may pass from his face when his attention is wholly absorbed by a moment of intense action on the part of his characters, yet as the crisis passes away it returns

and gleams again. After reading Scott, one feels the
same healthy happiness and elevation of spirit that
follow a run on the hill-side or an hour of merry work
with the gun or angle.

But this geniality is as direct an outcome of Scott's
personality as his delight in deeds of *derring-do* was the
result of his Border descent. Not Burns himself, with
all his hearty compassion for the wounded hare, and
'the wee timorous beastie,' the farmer's old mare, and
the 'hoggie,' was fuller of love for every kind of life
than Scott. Authentic stories show that even the
dumb beasts—not only the gallant staghounds and
terriers in which his soul delighted, but other creatures
—the frisky little pig that would follow him to the
hunt, the hen that embarrassed him with affection—
seemed instinctively to divine the man's universal and
kindly love. In their own dumb way they bore testimony to his goodness of heart as eloquently as did the
affection of Tom Purdie, of Willie Laidlaw, Shortreed,
Leyden, Hogg and many others, whose love for Scott is
their title to immortality. But this was nearly the most
prominent feature in his character. It shone brilliantly
during the period when he had to act host to 'sixteen
parties a day' at Abbotsford, sinking his own personality altogether out of sight, and gently directing the
conversation to the topics that interested his guests;
you see it in the pleasure he found during the most
active period of his life in 'serving some poor devil of
a brother author'; there is nothing in that last Journal
of his more affecting than his lament over the misfortunes heaped by fate on those whom he had helped.
His serene good-nature is exemplified again and again.
See him with a bunch of feathers playfully scourging

the irate Leyden, who had threatened to 'thraw the
neck of Ritson'; or receiving Jeffrey (after the critic's
onslaught upon *Marmion*), not only with high-bred
courtesy, but without abatement of his usual cordiality;
look at the measures taken for providing man and beast
at Abbotsford with one day of perfect rest in seven, and
you cannot doubt his amiability.

In his attitude towards his contemporaries the native
generosity of Scott's mind comes out in strong light.
There is no calling wherein that virtue finds a less congenial soil than in literature. Not only are envy and
jealousy and spite nourished by its rivalries, but no
other animosity is so deep as that germinated by a
difference in matters intellectual. Wordsworth stood
in need of no paltry or ulterior motive to make him
scorn the work of Byron, and Byron would have had a
genuine dislike of Southey without the stimulation of
any Scotch reviewer. Authors too frequently act as if
glory, influence, and wealth were prizes in a wrestling
match, wherein the athlete is victorious only if he casts
his opponents. There is hardly an important writer
belonging to the century that has not been associated
with strife and bickering, and the very names of those
most prominent in Scott's time, or who were fast rising
into prominence, are associated with feuds as bitter,
though not so sanguinary, as those between Guelf and
Ghibelline. Some, like Jeffrey and Gifford and
Wilson, were engaged in open warfare; others like
Carlyle wrote on private tablets, or spoke in private
talk, words that stung and rankled; a few like Lord
Tennyson, who links the two generations, would fain
have kept aloof, had not the bitter taunts levelled at
their work tempted them into the arena to break

a lance with 'crusty Christopher' or would-be Timon.

It was neither from disdain, nor from lack of pugnacity that the greatest of them all kept out of the fray. On more than one occasion Scott showed himself not only willing but eager to splinter a lance for political principles; and in his fifty-seventh year, broken down with pain, misfortune, and premature old age, the staunch Borderer's comment on the vapourings of General Gourgaud, who had taken umbrage at certain portions of the life of *Buonaparte*, was: 'At my years it is somewhat late for an affair of honour, and as a reasonable man I would avoid such an arbitrament, but will not plead privilege of literature. The country shall not be disgraced in my person, and having stated why I think I owe him no satisfaction, I will at the same time most willingly give it him.' But indeed it is the height of superfluity to adduce a single fact in proof of the noble courage of Scott, for the closing fight of his life is the most memorable example of fortitude in literature. There were two reasons, however, for his not quarrelling with brother artists. One was that he had no theory to defend. He worked without stopping to analyse his own mental processes, and did not call himself the prophet of a new movement. Suppose he had been living just now, it is easy to imagine with what genial irony he would have laughed away the cloudy warfare between Realist and Romanticist and Symbolist and Decadent, or with what infinite humour he would have observed the assurance with which critics who cannot create try to teach those who can. But the fact that his own energy and enthusiasm were expended on performance left him with only a languid interest in criticism. The man who actually does anything seldom cares to explain to himself how he accomplished it; but he whose success is questionable is naturally anxious to be convinced in his own mind, as well as to convince others, that although there might be flaws in the workmanship the idea was correct. In addition, Scott had no very high or exalted opinion of his own work, and a somewhat contemptuous one of the public that bought it, and his keenest interest lay outside the range of literary squabbles.

His greatest safeguard, however, was his own kindly disposition. While the estimation in which he held his own work continually erred on the side of over-modesty, his generous admiration for that of others was unlimited. Byron undoubtedly vanquished him for the time in his first field, that of romantic poetry, yet if a new piece from his hand had appeared it was sure to be read by Scott the Sunday evening afterwards, and that with such delighted emphasis as showed how completely the elder bard had kept all his enthusiasm for poetry at the pitch of youth, all his admiration of genius free, pure, and unstained by the least drop of literary jealousy. Wordsworth, Southey, Crabbe, and Hogg were among his close personal friends. Burns he looked up to as his humblest admirer might have done, and even accepted Joanna Baillie as the genius of her age. At the expense of his own 'great bow-wow' style he eulogised 'the fine domestic analysis of Jane Austen.' Indeed there was no author, either celebrated or obscure, who could complain of harsh judgment such as Carlyle passed on nearly every one of his contemporaries, or even of a bitter retort like the well-justified verses with which Alfred Tennyson repaid the snappish insolence

of Bulwer Lytton. The nearest approach he ever made
to acerbity was in the employment of a dry Scottish
irony, such as is brilliantly exemplified in his own
Jonathan Oldbuck, but which he delighted to introduce into nearly all his novels—Wamba, the son of
Witless, and 'Jinglin' Geordie,' Edie Ochiltree and
the immortal Bailie being at times mouthpieces of its
different phases. Yet of cynicism Scott is as guiltless
as Homer. The spirit of love and feasting, and
laughter and fun is in all his works, but his characters struggle and labour with frank sincerity towards
objects they never affect to hold in contempt. In that
sense he is the most earnest of writers, and never conceived of a hero who could turn with a merciless *cui
bono*, and pour scorn and ridicule upon the everlasting
chase of a woman, the greed of fame and other virtues
reduced by modern philosophy to the level of mere
incidents in a struggle for existence.

The quantity of himself that is in Scott's work
becomes the more apparent the more it is studied, and
had Lockhart possessed a tithe of the wizard's craft,
his long-winded narrative, over which so much mis-
directed admiration has been wasted, might have been
condensed into the essence of all the *Waverley Novels*.
For which of Scott's heroes will you not find a germ in
the early chapters of his own biography? The youth, of
which those of Allan Fairford and Lovel were the
closest variants, was spent in Edinburgh and Sandyknowe. Is not his typical young man dreamy and
poetical and fond of sport, game to the heels, eager for
adventure and quixotically honourable, of moderate
scholastic attainments, yet widely if not deeply read in
literature? There is not a hero of Scott's who is not

also a romantic lover; but his imagination never bodied forth a passion so deep and enduring as the hopeless affection that in the vigour of twenty-five he had, amid the birks of Inverury, nursed for Miss Stuart, and that still thrilled and moved him in dark later days, when most of his early acquaintances had 'one by one crept silently to rest,' and the mother of his children lay in the ruins of Dryburgh, while himself with palsied arm was fighting with overwhelming misfortune. It was by the light of that experience he saw how to make his lovers 'sigh like a furnace,' and understood the unspoken regret that encircles the stately and matchless Rebecca of his *Ivanhoe*. And the minor incidents through which he passes his heroes, the lone journeys, the dinners and drinking-bouts, the adventures at inn and hostelry, are but expanded or adapted from his own amusing expeditions to the Highlands or the Borderland.

Even the magical success of his books, the unparalleled sums of money he drew from the publishers, and the splendour of the fame that followed, look more as if they had been taken from a work of fiction than like sober fact. The ambition that grew from them was as logical a result of the man's character as were his novels. Nowhere does Carlyle write with such complete lack of understanding as when he contemptuously describes Scott 'writing daily with the ardour of a steam-engine that he might make £15,000 a year and buy upholstery with it. To cover the walls of a stone house in Selkirkshire with nicknacks, ancient armour and genealogical shields, what can we name it but a being bit with a delirium of a kind?' It is surprising how often that foolish judgment has in one form or another been repeated.

Although Carlyle was himself a Borderer it is easy to see why he failed to comprehend how Scott's ambition was natural to his temperament. For Carlyle was a schoolman pure and simple, a student, a book-worm, a theorist, one who never had 'gone the pace' even in lusty youth; who would hardly have known a stag-hound from a terrier; who never 'burned the water,' nor angled; who did not shoot nor hunt; and who consequently could not in the slightest degree enter into Scott's passion for sport. Yet if you were to imagine the great novelist without that, you could not conceive of his tales ever having been written. Indeed, a moment's reflection will show that no brood-ing recluse like Carlyle, or Mr. Ruskin, for example, could under any circumstances have invented anything like them. Scott's views of life came directly from Nature; those of his great critic from books; and it was not the man who lived, but he who only looked on and reflected, that showed signs of ill-health. When a man has the tastes of a country gentleman it is a natural desire that he should win for himself an estate; and if the creator of Jonathan Oldbuck had not as soon as he possessed stone walls collected within them 'a fouth o' auld nick-nackets' it would have indeed been strange.

Besides all this we have reason to be thankful for Scott's ambition, for without it he probably never would have troubled to convert his experience into art. Of Shakespeare, Carlyle himself says, 'had the War-wickshire squire not prosecuted him for deer-stealing we had perhaps never heard of him as a poet. The woods and skies, the rustic life of man in Stratford, these had been enough for this man.' If Scott had inherited greater wealth he would probably have fished and ridden, set the table in a roar with his merry jests and passed from memory as completely as many another rich Yorick. His itch for scribbling might have led to the composition of some dry antiquarian dissertation, but he valued literary fame so lightly that it never would have supplied a lasting impetus to his energy. The Abbotsford of his imagination, the ideal house and estate that he tried to realise, was the wages for which this labourer was willing to work; and from all his tastes and habits you could have predicted that it would be his choice; it falls in so harmoniously with the nature of the man.

The only mistake made by Scott lay in adding to the occupations of a lawyer, a literary man, and a stirring country gentleman the anxieties of business. If he had forsaken everything else he might have made an excellent publisher, for he had all the necessary sense, shrewdness, and ability; but there is a limit to the widest capacity, and the prolonged agony of Scott's last years was the merciless punishment inflicted by Nature for the innocent error. Fortunately it does not lie within our scope to trace the chain of events that led to Constable's bankruptcy and the rest of the troubles, or to describe one by one the steps by which disease advanced to death.

By the publication in full of his Diary attention has been to a very unhealthy extent directed to the sadness of Scott's later years. We are all familiar with the affecting incident in the life of Burns when the poor gauger, low in spirits and in health, was seen by Mr. M'Culloch walking alone on the shady side of the principal street of Dumfries, unnoticed by the prosper-

ous smiling men and gaily dressed women on the other
side, and how, when asked by this acquaintance to cross
the street, he replied, 'Nay, nay, my young friend, that's
all over now,' and then quoted some lines from Lady
Grizel Baillie's ballad :—

> ' His bonnet stood ance fu' fair on his brow,
>   His auld ane looked better than mony ane's new :
>   But now he let's wear ony gate it will hing,
>   And casts himself dowie upon the corn bing.
>
>   Oh, were we young as we ance ha' been,
>   We sud hae been gallopin' down on yon green,
>   And linking it ower the lily white lea—
>   And werena my heart light, I wad dee.'

There is a passage in the Diary equally touching, and
it runs as follows :—' Rode out, or more properly was
carried out, into the woods to see the course of a new
road which may serve to carry off the thinnings of the
trees and for rides.   It is very well lined and will serve
both for beauty and convenience.   Mr. Laidlaw engages
to come back to dinner and finish two or three more
pages.   Met my agreeable and lady-like neighbour, Mrs.
Brewster, on my pony, and I was actually ashamed to
be seen by her :—

> ' "Sir Denis Brand ! and on so poor a steed !" '

This perfectly natural emotion ought to have been
more fully respected.   Life has episodes from which every
vulgar, prying eye should be excluded.   Critics who
flush with indignation whenever a biting word is cast
at a contemporary, and who righteously declaim
against the modern love of gossip and personal detail,
have never raised a voice against the profanation of a
strong man's waning years.   Scott, in Lord Tennyson's

vigorous phrase, has been 'ripped up like a pig' and no protest made.

Their anger is wrongly directed. One honest man's frankly expressed opinion of another never can and never will do harm. If true, it cannot be too widely known; if false, it will do little and only a transitory damage before its falsehood is exposed. Nor is it entirely uninstructive to examine the intimate daily life of a great man and compare his written with his private revelation of character. But the Diary is a feast for ghouls and vampires. Paralysis is upon every page of it, to deepen the note of despair that comes from a man whose loved ones are lost, whose ambition is thwarted, whose projects are ruined, whose best hopes are buried. No doubt Scott's valiant struggle against so many adversities deserved chronicling, but that could have been done without losing dignity and force through being brief. At any rate it was wholly unnecessary to violate the sanctity of decay by bringing all the world to gaze on poor Sir Denis and his steed, to listen to his moanings and his maunderings, and set at naught the shame he felt at being so exhibited. Even the wild fox when he hears the limping tread of Death creeps to his most secluded earth, as if instinctively feeling that he should meet his grisly foe in secret, and the natural man shares something of the same desire.

What it is of high service to learn in Scott's life is not how one faculty of his mind after another gradually broke up, but how its noon-day splendour sprang into being and waxed in might. The birth and development of his genius form the theme of a story that can never fail to be fascinating; but the fact of the modern Borderer meeting misfortune and disease valiantly and with resolution is one that was inevitable from his character and lineage and traditions; and how a man lived is of far more importance to us than the manner of his death; more particularly so when the sum-total of his work has been to paint for us the romance of life.

V

LABORARE EST ORARE

(CARLYLE)

THOMAS CARLYLE was as essentially a Borderer as Sir Walter, but of an exactly opposite type. The ancestors of the novelist were brave knights and fair ladies who had tasted the adventures and made the romance of the marches, who played for great stakes in war, and in peace hunted the wild deer or idled away the hours with feasting and minstrelsy; those of the essayist were the rugged and lawless servitors who nominally followed a chieftain, but actually, like Hal o' the Wynd, fought each 'for his ain hand,' in battle more intent on robbing the vanquished than on supporting a side. If the pricker had any cause for pride it was in the swift nag that could traverse quagmire or morass as lightly as a bird, or his wife whom he made gay with the trinkets he had stolen. His remaining possessions were of the poorest: a miserable hut, which he unthatched and fled from at the approach of an enemy; a few head of cattle, now altogether lost, anon multiplied by the proceeds of a raid; a hound, and perhaps a hawk. When his life was not excited by feud or diversion there was plenty of mean shifting for his living; when the chieftain's wife cried, 'Hough 's i' the pot,' or showed a pair of clean spurs for dinner, it may be assumed that there was not much in the retainer's larder.

When peace and order were at last established in Borderland, and the moss-trooper was reluctantly obliged to doff forever his steel cap and his plate sleeves, he took very unkindly to the prosy dull labour of the fields. Even yet the villager of Annandale and Redesdale rebels against earning his bread by toil. In communities such as Ecclefechan, which is a fair sample of hundreds that lie on either side of the Solway and the Tweed, there is still a larger proportion of ne'er-do-weel wastrels than there is in any other district of Great Britain. Men like Carlyle's grandfather were very common a generation ago, and although school-boards and agricultural depression have forced the majority into the ranks of labour or of crime, a few still are left; but it is always a matter of chance under which lord they enlist. Generations of fierce and vigilant warfare have developed a tremendous energy which is apt to carry them to the utmost point of any path on which they start. Old Thomas Carlyle's exertions were, fortunately for himself, confined within a very small area. You may fancy him constantly living on the furthest outskirts of the lawful and not unseldom overstepping the boundary. Brawling at fair and market, an authority at dog and cock fights, probably the possessor of some unutterably game terrier or invincible fowl, a midnight poacher and a noted pugilist; 'proud, poor, and discontented,' says his grandson, careless of family comfort, leaving his children to scramble as they might for clothes and food; his home a half-way house for the itinerants with whose appearance the pencil of Bewick has made us familiar.

In a cottage that was place of call for the blind man and his dog, the peddler and packman and tinker, the clockie and the highland drover, it may be assumed that there were Saturday nights as wild and uproarious as 'gangrel bodies' ever made in the cot of Pousie Nancy. Nor is it at all out of keeping that the rough careless Bohemian was what his neighbours would call a great reader, a student of Anson's *Voyages*, and one who found a solace for old age in the *Arabian Nights*.

The fact of the Borders having produced the two greatest literary men of the century is proof enough that the barbaric wildness of the district is not inimical to culture. But had there never been any Scott or Carlyle it would still have been patent that the people have an innate love of poetry; how could it be otherwise where for generations the grandame at her spinning wheel crooned the most exquisite ballads extant to the children round the hearth? It has its ludicrous side no doubt, and it were easy to make fun of the drunken Northumbrian carter, who in his cups spouts 'On, Stanley, on!' or a choice bit of Byron, and the wastrels who, hardly able to stand, reel off the sonorous lines of Thomson. The love of literature thus evinced was in truth one of the most productive. A labouring man who has free access to newspapers and books grows as fluent and glib and shallow as the most commonplace cockney or city clerk, but he has no mental freshness left, and his ideas speedily are as worn and threadbare as those of a newspaper hack. But in the neglected Border villages, where no one used to care a jot whether a man read or not, books were very scarce, and came to those who could appreciate them as rare and peculiar luxuries. A man who poached and drank and swore, who never went to church, and as often as he had money to the public-house, nevertheless took a genuine delight in such thumbed and mutilated books as came into his possession; and I am probably safe in asserting that nowhere else in England or Scotland are there so many full book-shelves in the homes of the very poorest portions of the population as in the Borders; and by books I do not mean religious tracts and Bible commentaries such as are found everywhere, but the works of Swift and Burns, of Eliza Cook and Cooper and Scott, Bunyan and the voyages of La Perouse, selecting at random from those I have seen. It is probably an outcome of the passionate love of adventure that is so cabined, cribbed, and confined by modern circumstances as to have no other outlet. In the case of Carlyle's grandfather it was evidently originated by the spontaneous and natural pleasure of sharing by imagination in adventures from which he was otherwise debarred; and it is of consequence to us as helping to explain the inherited tastes of the author of *Sartor Resartus*.

It was into the singular household of this typical old Borderman that James Carlyle, the father of Thomas, was born, and his early experience was a rough one. Ill clothed, ill fed, thrust into wild company, obliged as soon as he was able to scramble for existence, to knit and thatch for money, to poach for dinner, it becomes difficult to see how he imbibed the notions of respectability by which his life was subsequently guided. Yet the change was easy and natural, for there was nothing hostile to religion and ambition in the family. The Carlyles were by nature destined to Puritanism.

Sour, bitter, and discontented in temper, they did not evince even in their wildest and most pagan days the untamed passions and generous vices of the prodigal, and their overbearing disposition and strenuous energy easily flowed into the new channel. The conversion of James was accomplished in a fashion highly characteristic of the Borders. In the medley of visitors to Thomas Carlyle's, who seems to have kept a common lodging-house at Brownknowe, was the drunken school-master of Hoddam, a clever man named Orr, who when in drink talked Bible as another rants poetry, and was ever most pious and repentant in his maudlin moments. James Carlyle, a boy of cold and solid sense, picked up the jewels dropped by this strange missionary with all the more alacrity inasmuch as he saw nothing inviting in the creed of his father or the absence of any creed. An accidental occurrence settled him permanently on the new path. There came from Peebles a mason named Brown who, marrying Fanny the eldest girl of the Burnswark household, offered to take her two brothers as apprentices, and James Carlyle, forsaking the unsettled and questionable life in which he had been brought up, settled himself down as a steady soldier in the ranks of industry. Though the old, moss-trooping spirit now and then led him into fierce quarrels, and won him the reputation of a hard striker, it did not interfere with the energetic pursuit of his task, so that his career was an example to boys of a new generation. At the expiration of his apprenticeship he and his brother—you always find the Carlyles sticking to one another like Border clansmen—commenced business on their own account, and built a joint house for themselves in Ecclefechan, to which, as the years began to weigh heavily on him, they brought the old heathen and his *Arabian Nights* from Brownknowe.

Thus before his marriage James Carlyle had raised himself clean out of the gutter, and Thomas was in due time born into a home of such comfort and success as falls to the lot of a village mason. Computed in money it was little, yet where thrift was an instinct and frugality a second nature it was abundance. When an English workman would be thinking of the workhouse a Scotsman will save money. As to the little and not very robust philosopher, he was early inured to the abstemiousness he subsequently taught, for sage and clodpole are as equal in the cradle as in the grave, and no light from the future shines on the mother dandling her baby. Peggy Carlyle was a Scotch wife of the best type. If her children were clean and comfortable she did not think of finery; if they had plenty of porridge they stood in no need of sweetmeats; and for the rest they had to run barefoot and sleep on chaff; yet when her apron was off and her housework done in the afternoon, the floor fresh sanded and a log on the fire, she taught them their letters, and at bedtime to pray. For she was in full sympathy with the keen religious enthusiasm that deepened in her husband with the establishment of his household. Every Sunday the boys were taken to the heath-thatched house where John Johnstone 'the simple evangelist' held a conventicle, and poured into them his good and earnest yet narrow teaching. This man Carlyle venerated to his last hour, and probably imbibed from him the germs of the Puritanism that coloured his teaching; for, of course, it is absurd to talk of him as though he were a product of the Presbyterianism of centuries. On the

CARLYLE

contrary, in the class of Borderers from which he sprung there was, after the fall of Catholicism, no religion whatever save that which took the form of gross superstition.

If, however, children can be induced to take an interest in such matters the teaching of one whom they love and who seems clothed with authority is more likely to take deep root than any that follows. At all events time was to show that the burning zeal of John Johnstone was to bear fruit in the life of another hearer, an eager, kind-faced boy with a cast in his eye, who in due time was to electrify London with his eloquence; for, as yet unknown to his future friend, Edward Irving was a worshipper with Carlyle.

It is abundantly plain that the doctrine of toil, which was the burden of Carlyle's teaching, not only originated at home but imperceptibly and unconsciously permeated its very atmosphere. James Carlyle, 'most quiet but capable of blazing into whirlwinds,' had concentrated and directed all the vast energy, which in a man of different temperament had been dissipated in wildness and devilment, upon one point, and that was to win and hold the countryman's ambition, an independence; his wife was a woman 'who looked upon toil as the natural occupation of her sex,' and who would have thought herself defrauded of a right if she were not allowed to scrub and wash and boil and bake; and you may be sure that if the minister enlarged upon one text more frequently than another it was that which afterwards became the favourite of his pupil, 'Whatsoever thy hand findeth to do, do it with thy might.' The atmosphere of the household was one that suited well with this hard, clear, and stern outlook

I

on life. You search in it for any evidence of trifling or amusement as vainly as in the pages of *Cromwell* or the *French Revolution*. The father is so cold, repellent, and taciturn as to be in a sense unknown to his children, and to waste words seems to have been held an offence equal to that of wasting money; the spirited mother alone had a vein of sport and liveliness in her disposition that under more favourable circumstances would have added a new charm to her many excellent qualities. But a stern religion taken with hard labour in unlimited quantities was a check upon that kind of brilliance.

It happened, however, that the boy was in perfect harmony with his environment, and what would have withered the genius of a Scott was food and nourishment to his. The plant grew apace because the soil was so well adapted to it. School was miserable, for the tall thin boy had little sympathy with the frolic gamesomeness of children, and was not companionable with the classmates, who after the manner of their kind bullied and persecuted the 'tainted wether of the flock' till he was driven into solitude and communion with his own thoughts. But he made progress with his studies, and his father having become enamoured of respectable life, and with all the fiery intensity of the race having embraced religion, as one of the strict and narrow sect of Burghers, conceived the idea of serving these two passions and capping his prosperity by attempting to realise a darling ambition of many a thriving Scottish peasant and preparing his son 'to wag his pow in a poopit.' For that purpose Carlyle, at the age of fourteen, was sent off to Edinburgh University, there to experience another phase of the frugal simplicity with which the perfervid genius of his countrymen is nourished.

Student life was a continuation of that at Ecclefechan. James Carlyle, who had known such famine that when meal came at length he and the rest rose in the middle of the night to feast on cakes baked with a fire of straw torn from under the beds, and who like some provident wild beast had once stored away four potatoes against want, had a philosophy of life with only two commands, that were in substance, 'Save your soul and work for your living.' These were the essentials, and the rugged strenuous family were taught to despise everything extraneous to them. None kept the precepts more in memory than the poor scholar, who one murky afternoon in November 1809 walked into Simon Square, Edinburgh, to begin study in earnest. Physically it was no pleasant change. The country boy gave up the rough plenty of home for a mean lodging where he and his friend slept two in a bed, and their food was a scrimped allowance of porridge, potatoes, and butter sent in by the carrier. From the wild and lurid pleasures of town they were protected by the emptiness of their pockets. University life, that means so much to the rich man's son, meant for the child of the ambitious mason hard fare and self-denial and constant application. Even on intellectual ground he competed on unfavourable terms with those of his rivals who came from more cultured families, who had attended better schools, and who had received the invaluable education that comes from intercourse with a cultivated domestic circle. Carlyle's early instruction at Hoddam Kirk School and Annan Academy had been neither thorough nor accurate, and was probably the cause of such mistakes as *omnibi* (for *omnes*) that gave his enemies a handle to the end of his career. Under the circumstances it would have been surprising if he had distinguished himself in his classes, and he speaks with contempt of what he received from any of the Professors except Leslie, who further developed the mathematical faculty that in early years seemed his strongest.

But the years were not wasted. Even if he had not said as much in *Sartor Resartus*, the records of the University Library would show how he plunged right and left into literature that lay far apart from the line of his formal studies. Philosophy, travel, drama, fiction, and poetry were absolutely devoured by the ardent lad, who must have at that time felt a striking contrast between the sedate little world he had known on the Scots' Borderland and the free and reckless one disclosed by Fielding, Smollett, and the rest of his first favourites in romance. Much as he owed to books, however, he owed no less to his college companions. 'No man quickeneth his own soul,' says the Psalmist, and quite as stimulating and suggestive as any lecture or exhortation is the nimble talk of fellow students, the quick and eager play of fresh and keen young minds. Among them we already see Carlyle's character exhibiting the stamp it had received at Ecclefechan. He is the prudent and frugal member of the community, the one who from the smallest dole of pocket-money will put by something for a rainy day, and already the overbearing combativeness that was to surprise the drawing-rooms of London, that was generated by his marauding ancestors, and that owing to his calling and *physique* had not the outlet of fisticuffs, for which his family were famous, began to exhibit itself in speech, the only ordeal of battle open to him. 'I would like to hear thee argue with him,' said his father to him, two years before he died, when they were talking of Jeffrey, proud of his son's prowess displayed in a field that did not make him 'wae to think on 't,' and one may easily gather that in such encounters, especially in early life, Carlyle found a certain joy of combat. Very bitter of tongue he could be, and 'far too sarcastic for so young a man,' but the lingual wrestling bouts, wherein he was dubbed the Dean, prepared him—thewing his mind as it were—for the intellectual athletics performed afterwards. Probably also the light, clever, half-scoffing conversation of his friends, in direct contrast with the earnest and serious talk of home, had its effects in turning him from a calling chosen for him without the manifestation on his own part of any love for it. At any rate we find him saying in one of his later letters—written at the age of nineteen—that, 'Ever since I have been able to form a wish, the wish of being known has been the foremost'; and again, 'O Fortune! . . . Grant me, that with a heart of independence unyielding to thy frowns, I may attain to literary fame; and though starvation be my lot, I will smile that I have not been born a king.' A country manse could hardly possess much attraction for a youth who enrolled himself so unreservedly among the worshippers of the 'goose-goddess.' But it was many a day ere he needed to make a final decision. According to the economical Scotch method candidates for the ministry are not expected to go straight through their course, and it used to be the common practice for students to fill in the intervening time with schoolmastering.

The most important feature in this period of his career is his friendship with Edward Irving, whose intersecting story for a time flashes in and about that of Carlyle, as one sometimes may see a sunny brook winding, racing, and glittering by the side of a dark railway. They had shared in Adam Hope's religious training, been taught by the same masters, and had grown up amid the same traditions and surroundings. Both were filled to overflowing with strong ambition, and both were born mystics. Here, however, the resemblance ended. In personal character they showed a marked contrast. The Irving of those days is a picture the mind delights to rest on, a full-blooded, laughing youth, rejoicing as youth should rejoice in the joy of life and the beauty of earth; distinguished he and his brother as boys at school for their wild love of sport as well as readiness in school lessons. As mathematical master at Annan you see Carlyle, then a lad of nineteen, a jealous recluse, saving money out of his sixty or seventy pounds a year, studying the reflection of life in books, carefully avoiding life itself as it lay around him, watching the career of the other brilliant Borderer with an eye from which the cold glow of malicious envy was excluded only by an effort of will. When they meet in Edinburgh 'victorious Irving,' with the regal, innocent vanity of young manhood, and its careless happy superiority, undreaming of the thoughts that are stirring in Thomas, is sharply rebuffed for imagining that his warm human interest in sickness and childbirth and death and marriage is as much the other's as his own. At their next forgathering it is the bitter-mouthed, doubting Carlyle who, suspicious as a dog that with stiff bristles watches a

stranger, expects a sour after-taste of the first *rencontre*;
all the more so because meanwhile he had been
appointed rival schoolmaster to Irving in Fife. But on
the latter's mind the disagreeable incident had made as
little impression as the cloud shadow that scuds over
yet hardly darkens a summer sea. 'My house and all
that I can do for you is yours,' said he. 'Two Annandale people must not be strangers in Fife.' And he
was as good as his word, 'exuberantly good' says
Carlyle. 'Upon all these you have your will and way-
gate,' he exclaimed, showing his books, and how sweet
and grateful this welcome was to the proud, struggling
Carlyle one may learn from his description of the night
or two he lodged with Irving, a description written
more than fifty years after and that shines with the
light of a happy memory: 'Bright moonshine; waves
all dancing and glancing out of window, and beautifully
humming and lullabying on that fine long sandy beach
where he and I so often walked and communed afterwards.'

So the foundation of this interesting friendship was
laid, and it was cemented during the years wherein
the two remarkable schoolmasters were companions to
one another on the smooth Kirkcaldy beach, in woodland rovings, and in excursions to Dysart, Wemyss,
Dunfermline, and other interesting places in Fifeshire.
Both were lovers of the open air, and the very differ-
ences of their dispositions gave them food for talk. In
society, or indeed wherever he met with his fellow-men,
the free-flowing, brotherly Irving is the favourite. He
was no bookworm, but yet 'with solid ingenuity and
judgment, by some briefer process of his own, fished
out correctly from many books the substance of what

they handled and of what conclusions they came to.'
This was supplemented by information at first-hand.
' He had gathered by natural sagacity and insight,' says
Carlyle, ' from conversation and inquiry, a great deal of
practical knowledge and information on things extant
round him, which was quite defective in me the recluse.'
Indeed, a more delightful companion than Edward
Irving was in these days imagination cannot conceive.
His laughter rang loud and happy, for he had not yet
felt the stress and strain of life, his bright ardour was
not yet compressed into the narrowing and mad enthusiasm of later life, his keen sense of the ludicrous was
edged by the vitality of youth, and his fine originality,
if unripened, was still at its most interesting stage,
while the innate goodness of heart that was always his
shed its beautiful radiance over every other quality.
Carlyle was a dark foil to all this geniality.   In place
of Irving's open and splendid ambition, there were below
his cold, sarcastic exterior unavowed aspirations, that
for the present produced only a discontent hardly
sufficient to set in motion the tremendous power and
energy of the man.   With all his reading he became
no mere student and bookworm, not even a great and
finished scholar, because his cold and piercing good
sense was fatal to vague theorisation.   Nor was he at
all a visionary.   Nearly all great literary men except
himself have been dreamers and idlers.   To muse and
brood, and live in reverie is in fact the primal stage of
creation.   But the imagination that gave Carlyle a constant supply of vivid image and glowing metaphor
inspires no hours of castle-building and fashioned no
fictitious adventures ; dreaming and idleness being in
fact objects of his abhorrence.   It was a want of faculty

that made itself felt when he came to attempt creative work; for he could not imagine a story. Neither could Irving for the matter of that, but then the preacher had built himself a new heaven and a new earth, and in fancy could people them as he liked.

In default of finding this outlet for his faculty, Carlyle's more inactive moments were apparently spent in a reverie of criticism. No equally eminent writer has so greatly concerned himself with the work of others. And he treats them all as if there were only one subject to be discussed. It is the business of the intellectual worker, he implies, to find and set forth symbolically or otherwise a theory for men's guidance, a rule for their conduct. You feel from his writings that even during these early Kirkcaldy days he was questioning the authors lent him by Irving upon those points. Irving's happier nature exulted in the pure buoyancy of life ; Carlyle could not do so. He was as one who hastening through green lanes for a physician will not dally a moment to look at the brook rippling through the waving hayfield, or the singing birds, and who feels only his own weakness as he pants uphill. Other men delight us with interludes of frolic playfulness, interrupting themselves as it were to chase butterflies on the sunny highway ; it seems a regret to him to waste five minutes in the indulgence of his sardonic humour. The strictest Burgher of Presbyterian Covenanter Scotland was not more completely divorced from the lusts of the flesh, and there never was apostle or missionary with ideas more concentrated on his message. His mind was essentially as pious as that of his mother, but reading and study and intercourse had for him obscured the landmarks that were her definite and accepted guide-posts. The one clear conviction remaining was that man was no mere insect, purposelessly called forth by the sunshine to flutter and play for an hour and then to die, to forget, and be forgotten, but a labourer in the vineyard of the Lord, with a task to be accomplished ere nightfall that would leave him no time for mere enjoyment. And with the Ram Dass fire of a marauding ancestry burning in his belly, and the religious zeal of a Scotch seceder, he fastened and concentrated himself upon this idea with a forced indifference to surroundings. 'Doesn't this subdue you, Carlyle?' asked Irving, as in an October dusk they stood together before the Falls of Aberfeldy. 'Subdue me? I should hope not. I have quite other things to front with defiance than a gush of bog-water tumbling over crags as here,' answered he to whom later the blue dome and its golden stars were 'a sair sicht.'

Nevertheless, that expressed no real sentiment, and in fact was meant only as corrective of a certain affectation in Irving's question, for Nature in the whole of this century has had no more ardent lover than the writer whom she reinvigorated after toil as he lay by the sunny dyke-backs at Ecclefechan. You may fancy the two friends more in unison during the autumn tramp among the pleasant Cheviots, where there is 'no company to you but the rustle of the grass underfoot, the tinkling of the brook, or the voices of innocent primeval things.' If it be noted how of every remarkable day, however long-distant, the weather, the clouds, and the sun have made an imprint on Carlyle's memory as deep as the event itself, it will be seen that if ever the stern moralist was tempted to waste his working hours, it was not by idle book, nor the joy of intercourse, but by spirits that haunt the shady lane and open moor, and never are quite absent where sky is the only ceiling of earth. He vividly remembers 'the red, sunny Whitsuntide morning' of his entry to Annan Academy; and to pass a thousand similar references, there is a passage in his Journal, dated October 14th, 1869, that is to say in his seventy-fifth year, which has an undercurrent of regret, disclosing, as it appears to me, though couched in reticent terms, a passionate love of earth as intense as that which Jefferies beggared his vocabulary to express. 'Three nights ago,' he writes, 'stepping out after midnight, with my final pipe, and looking up into the stars, which were clear and numerous, it struck me with a strange new kind of feeling. Hah! in a little while I shall have seen you also for the last time. God Almighty's own Theatre of Immensity, the Infinite made palpable and visible to me, that also will be closed, flung to in my face, and I shall never behold that either any more, and I know so little of it, real as was my effort and desire to know. The thoughts of this external deprivation—even of this, though this is nothing in comparison—was sad and painful to me.'

The student of minute life wept that the orchis flower would blow, and the chaffinch build, that the forget-me-not would follow the violet, and the water-lilies bloom when the iris had faded, while he who did it so lovingly was no longer there to keep the calendar for them. And even Shakespeare, who was less of a rustic than either of them, knew by name and loved all the small familiar gems of field and hedgerow; but it is to the stars that the thoughts of the great Transcendentalist journey and return. 'There is a majesty and mystery

in Nature,' he wrote to Miss Welsh from Mainhill, 'take
her as you will. The essence of all poetry comes
breathing to a mind that feels from every province of
her empire. Is she not immovable, eternal, and
immense in Annandale as she is in Chamouni? The
chambers of the East are opened in every land, and
the sun comes forth to sow the earth with orient pearl.
Night, the ancient mother, follows him with her diadem
of stars; and Arcturus and Orion take me into the
Infinitudes of space as they called the Druid priest or
the shepherd of Chaldea. Bright creatures! how they
gleam like spirits through the shadows of immeasurable ages from their thrones in the boundless depths of
Heaven :—

> ' " Who ever gazed upon them shining,
> And turned to earth without repining,
> Nor wished for wings to fly away
> To mix with their ethereal day." '

When Nature, as she always did, soothed his jarring
nerves and revived his weary mind he made no close
inquiry into the apparatus she employed. As the fitful
summer breeze, bending the tall grass stalks over the
lowlier opening clover, made glistening, wandering islets,
he loved the effect, and was careless of the cause;
whether it was skua or sea-mew winging its flight
above the white-crested wavelets breaking on the coast
was indifferent to him; facts like these it did not come
within his province to gather. Indeed he was habitually unjust to those who, straying as it were in the by-
paths of art and life, forgot what he esteemed their high
calling, and fashioned things that were merely beautiful.
That you could read Scott lying on the sofa was enough
to condemn him; Petrarch was an idle sonneteer; even

the gentle Elia ' a pitiful, rickety, gasping, staggering, stammering Tomfool.' For all men who were not doing practical work, or trying to solve the great mystery of existence, he had something of that abhorrence that Praise-God-Barebones felt for scented cavaliers, play-actors, and the Scarlet Woman. He lived in strict accordance with a stern rule of his fathers : 'As we spend our time here so will our eternal state be.' It is by performing the will of God that we come near him ; it is by labouring that we pray. Due intervals of rest have indeed been appointed wherein the kindly mother of life smiles on her children with sunshine, and fans them with the refreshing wind, and spreads before their eyes her pictures of green and gold ; but these are only meant as solace to the toiler. He is but an idle and unprofitable servant who loiters where enjoyment is, and seeks his pleasure while the task he was sent to accomplish remains undone. That was the gist of Carlyle's bitter onslaught upon Sir Walter and his like. The author of *Waverley* was strictly an artist who bartered in pleasure, giving light intellectual amusement to his readers in return for certain broad acres and ' a stone house in Selkirkshire with nicknacks.'

It is a creed that has fallen out of vogue with the more general acceptance of evolutionary principles. A modern critic has indeed named the doctrine of toil ' a modern heresy,' and asserts that Nature knows nothing of it. But this is a contradiction in terms, for man is as truly a part of Nature as any bird that forages the woodlands for its slender meal and then flutes its satisfaction from the spray; and his ships that have not left a bit of all the wide blue sea unploughed, his engines that scream along the mountain flanks, his bridges spanning great inlets of the sea attest the truth of his description as the 'worker,' even though this apparent madness for toil were but an exaggeration of the sentiment that makes the ant with heavy labour drag the grains of wheat to his hillock, and the wild bee gather her honey, and the squirrel his little hoard of nuts. But Carlyle would have rejected with scorn this translation of the monkish legend. He who cared so much for truth and so little for wages, he who was so earnest and frugal and averse to luxury, who was so scornful of the scramble for 'hog's wash,' whose rage for truth and hatred of sham was so pure and noble, could all his high imaginings and soaring speculations be reducible to this? Nay, was it possible for him to have endured all the travail and sorrow of the thirteen years he took to write *Frederick*, all the long toil of *Cromwell* and the *French Revolution*, if his only inspiration had been a hope of personal reward? With his extraordinary energy, piercing insight, vivid imagination, and brilliant humour, there were at his disposal a hundred easier means of gaining bread and even winning smiles from 'the goose-goddess.'

It cannot be assumed that Carlyle was indifferent to these incentives. The village mason's son knew the value of money as only a poor man does, and several of his finest essays were written primarily because he needed it. And he had also a considerable love of fame, as one may see, not only from his early and natural aspirations, but from many incidents of his later career, as, for example, his gratification at being chosen Lord Rector of Edinburgh University. He recognised, too, how this passion, strongest always in the strongest men, had shaped the destiny of heroes, and led to some of the most significant events in history. But for the sake of either the one or the other he would not swerve from his own high purpose. His guide and exemplar, Goethe, though towards the end of his life he said if he were young he would study to have something to say rather than how to say it—thus fully endorsing the view of Carlyle—was the most perfect literary artist of his time. But Carlyle despised *Kunst*, and hardly knew what was meant by art for art's sake. His method was simply to wrestle himself into a strong clear grasp of his idea, and then to set it forth with all the force of which he was capable. And yet he had much that goes to make up the intellectual equipment of an artist. Expression was an instinct with him. Some men of a different temperament try to pass silently and unostentatiously through the world: impressions, thoughts, dreams, ideas travel in continuous procession through the mind, but no record is kept of their appearance; petty troubles and pains and annoyances go noiselessly by; grief itself produces but a sadder quiet. It was not so with the voluble Carlyle. In talk he was loud and ceaseless, and a letter writer who posted an essay to each correspondent, while many of his essays stretch out to the length of a treatise and his books engulf space. Not only so, but the writer of *Characteristics* was the most self-conscious of men. It is not so much that every little stomach-ache and petty disturbance, every crowing cock and barking dog and undigested dinner makes him vocal, but he is for ever taking out, handling, and considering his inmost emotions. Who but one to whom writing was second nature could have sat down between the death and burial of a passionately loved father and examined,

described, and analysed the bond that had been between
them ?   Moreover he could hardly see a strange face
or new scene without describing it, and that with so
much of general effect and absolute clearness of detail
as proved that doing this roused his intellect to its
keenest and most intense activity.   Were all his morali-
sations and prophecies to become non-extant to-morrow,
his pictures of men and places would still ensure him
a high place in English literature.

The artist's faculty of taking pains he possessed to
the highest degree.   As with Goethe 'nothing came to
him in his sleep,' and at his ruggedest moment he is
not to be classed with the slovenly philosopher who is
content to pitchfork his ideas to the public formless.
'No great thing was ever, or ever will be done with
ease, but with difficulty,' he wrote, in reference to Scott.
' Let ready-writers with any faculty in them lay this to
heart.   Is it with ease, or not with ease, that a man
shall *do his best* in any shape ; above all in this shape
justly named of "soul's travail"?'   In the same spirit
he accounts for the *longueurs* of Diderot.   ' It is said "he
wrote good pages, but could not write a good book."
Substitute *did not* for *could not*; and there is truth in
the saying.'   Carelessness in this respect indeed roused
in him an anger equal to that of his father when he
told an incorrigibly bad shearer, 'Thou maun alter thy
figure or slant the bog,' bad workmanship being equally
hateful to both.   If Carlyle made a mistake in this
respect it lay in his being too careful.   Mrs. Carlyle
was of opinion that his best work was that done quickly ;
and the *Reminiscences*, composed almost extemporane-
ously, show by their exquisitely beautiful and simple
diction that elaboration may at times be advantageously

dispensed with. Yet it did not lead him at any time into being florid or 'precious,' which are the growing vices of our literature. He had a genuine love of words—displayed no less in his taste for philology than in his copious and significant vocabulary—but he had also a keen appreciation of the critic's crabbed rule:— 'Whenever you have written any sentence that looks particularly excellent be sure to blot it out.' You may search his pages long enough before discovering a single gleam of false or merely glittering rhetoric. Despite the unmeasured profusion of his writing, every sentence has the strength and vivacity of a line of Burns. Whatever be the faults of Carlyle, there never is any doubt of his surpassing intellectual vigour, his un-questioned honesty, his fiery blazing zeal.

Nevertheless, in spite of this splendid equipment, Carlyle would not try to be an artist in prose composi-tion. Whether his diction was pure or not, or whether the picture was complete, caused him no solicitude. Every piece of work he had to do was planned, not to be a completed and interesting structure, but to develop the lesson or morality that lay at the heart of it; and if, as the Darwinian says, his teaching was based on a false authority, if, for example, the difference between right and wrong be no eternal antagonism but only a convenient arrangement, then the works of Carlyle are already fading before truth and are doomed to fade.

For the moment indeed materialism has cast its paralysis on literature, and has made great poetry or great writing of any kind impossible, and there are some who prophesy that all who belong to the era that came before the new cosmogony are hurrying to oblivion ; that light is dawning on a new day for literature. It is an unsafe inference. Human nature is not to be revolutionised by scientific discovery, and there is nothing in evolution to cut off the dim possible belief beyond which Shakespeare himself does not appear to have ventured, 'There's a Divinity that shapes our ends.' Nor does it seem probable that any man in any age who has been free from the dogma customarily wound round the plastic mind of youth ever believed much more, while every student of the lives of saint and confessor, early father and pilgrim and hermit, has come across words and phrases to show that the holiest of them in his heart of hearts looked out on a vaguer 'beyond' than his strict creed might suggest. The mistake made to-day lies in the comfortable and somewhat lazy assumption that the mystery has all been swept aside and facts bared to their hard outline; an assumption upon which much French and some English literature is founded, but for which knowledge offers no warranty.

'We bid you to hope'; that was what Carlyle judged most important to tell the young students; and it was the repeated consolation of his last years. No competent modern man of science—not Darwin nor Pasteur nor Tyndall nor even Huxley—has sought to prove that the exhortation is based on insufficient data; that the origin and end of life and the phenomenon of consciousness are so clearly defined and known as to change hope into a fixed certainty. But the majority of men will always be either old priest or new presbyter. They will believe him who roundly affirms a heaven with gold paven streets, hell smoking and flaming, legions of evil fiends in torment, white-clothed angels singing in companies. Prove that this vision is not to say the least, a fully assured truth and the ordinary mind flies to the other extreme, and life is but a form of heat, the complex body an avenue shapen by force to escape from a cooling planet, and we like insects that flutter for an hour in the sunshine and then are annihilated. The really great men of the past, whether they lived in times of gross superstition or open unbelief, have rushed to neither extreme. Whoever has even for a moment forgotten all the teaching and tradition of church and school in close and uninterrupted communion with Nature has lost the full and clear assurance of this or that superstition, but retains a frail, fine glimpse of Hope.

Carlyle adopted the stirring and dignified hypothesis, that the working of the universe is informed with purpose, that, come how it may, good in the end must be the final goal of ill; and if this be true, *Laborare est orare* is not the stern incredible creed it would appear. Surely, though it pinned one to the task of a galley slave, though it drove brightness and laughter from existence, one would rather work towards the fulfilment of a great purpose than reconcile one's-self to be a moving fungus, generated by moisture and heat, and resolvable again to dust and ashes. But the alternative is not so harsh. If Nature has called on men to toil, she has provided rest and pleasure for them also, and bestows the fullest draughts of them on the weary. Carlyle himself, in spite of his earnestness and lamentation, had of merry laughing hours as good a share as the most, hours like that told of by Professor Masson, when on the evening after the Rectorial distress, his rough voice joined in the chorus 'Stuart Mill on mind and matter.' And in spite of dyspepsia he had frequent

tastes of the full and quiet joy defined by himself as
'the only true happiness of a man, that of clear decided
activity in the sphere for which by Nature and circumstances, he has been fitted and appointed.'

Labour such as this is as sweet to Nature as the lark's
orisons are to the ear of the shepherd, and she has no
treasure she will not lavish on the worshipper who
makes of it his prayer.   For strength and encouragement she pours him forth a wine more exhilarating
than any that ever flowed from an ivy-leaved chalice ;
she blesses him with health and strength of body, and
from all the mad distractions and idle sorrows of the
world protects him within an olive grove of content-
ment and peace and retains her choicest laurel wreath
for his head.   The only man to be envied, the only
man who rightly knows what pleasure is, is he who has
discovered his task and is doing it.

But ere he win her approbation the labourer must be
as wise as he is industrious, and she punishes with care
and pain and sickness the mad fury of those who work
beyond a limit strictly reasonable.   The element of
extragavance that lay in Carlyle, the exaggeration inherited from his father, brought punishment upon him.
Writing *Frederick* was to him a joyless slavery, but it
was a task rashly conceived and undertaken, producing
ultimately neither pleasure nor satisfaction ; done with
an ill-judged and dogged perseverance that neither
commands our admiration, nor was crowned with
the glory of perfect achievement.   In work there are
extremes as harmful as any that reside in idleness,
and in some cases it produces a kind of delirium that
is mother to misleading phantoms.   When directed, for
example, to the inordinate amassing of gold, or inspired

by a greedy lust of fame, not only is its dignity lost, but pleasure flies from it, and the semblance only of reward is yielded to its votaries. Riches are not gathered till the capacity to enjoy them is past, nor celebrity attained till its glory has faded, till those whose knowledge and share of it formed half its value are dead, till the man feels as lonely as a shipwrecked sailor standing by chests of gold in a land untenanted.

Carlyle's error, if error it was, differs from those in arising from disinterested love of his fellow-men. It was because he prized so highly the virtues experience has declared of value to the human race, that he nerved himself for new labour at a time of life when others are thinking of rest. If he over-estimated the necessity of preaching morality, if he was too obstreperous at times in the denunciation of sham and pretence, too loud and arrogant in his continual insistance on what he reckoned to be truth and integrity, we still have more cause of gratitude than anger. For his was a good and generous instinct, and without under-estimating any of his contemporaries, it is permissible to say that the nineteenth century would have been poorer and flabbier without the presence and work of this valiant Borderman. His noble, rugged courage and perseverance, his strong championship of the true against the false, his piercing scornful denunciation of pretence and sham, even the unequalled laughter of his brighter hours, form his claim to a place among the greatest men produced out of the Saxon race.

VI

THE POETRY OF TOIL

(BURNS)

BETWEEN the present time and that of William
Shakespeare, it is strange that the most buoyantly
humorous verse should have come from a peasant; that
a line of labouring ancestors should have flowered into
a triumph of mirth which, though mingled with tears,
is the strongest and most catching in our language.
Literature usually paints in gloomy colour the lowest
grades of honest society. To say nothing of M. Zola's
French coal-pit, which looks as if it had been drawn to
outrival the hell of Dante, or the grimy pictures of
younger novelists, who like him go to slums for material, it is noticeable that the most genial and catholic
of writers seldom unlock the cottage door save to discover a vision of want, or an embodiment of stupidity
or discontent. Even Shakespeare's frolic fancy, though
it people the sunny glades of Arden with joyous wits
and melancholy humourists from court, finds only a
target for ridicule in the boorish natives; and elsewhere
in his stately dramas, though jester and king, lady and
soldier and priest have their mirthful moments, the
poor clown is introduced only to be laughed at. It is
meat and drink for the author to meet him, and he

quizzes and bemocks the spectacle, as we may suppose
him to have done when, travelling as a lad on his
father's business to Cirencester, he fell in with the
simple Cotswold shepherds. Sir Walter too reserves
his brightest merriment and pleasantry for the
educated and well-to-do. Isabella Wardour would
perhaps deny it in jealous championship of the gaber-
lunzie, but Edie is really a gentleman at ease who begs
as a pastime, and who is a counsellor of lovers and
keeper of secrets. The sturdy and faithful, yet sullen
and discontented, Gurth is a more typical example
of Scott's toiler. Cervantes indeed took Sancho from
a cottage, but he laughs at his squire as heartily as
Shakespeare could have done, or as Fielding does at
poor Partridge with his *Infandum regina jubes renovare
dolorem.* As to Thackeray, the peasant's hut lay quite
outside the genteel world of his knowledge, and the
poor whom Dickens immortalised were cockneys.

Nevertheless, all the poets from Theocritus down to
Gray and Wordsworth have told us how blithe is the
milkmaid at her pail, how jocund the ploughman as he
drives his team a' field; how Corydon on his pipe of
oaten straw blows music sweeter than Pan draws from
the reeds, how Strephon's singing has a stronger charm
than the lute of Orpheus. Imagination has clothed
every incident of rural life with a garment of symbol-
ism, parable, and verse, and their continual use by poets
has invested the common words of the farm with more
than their primal meaning. The scythe and the sickle,
the spade and the ploughshare, are used as much in
poetry as in field-work, and seed-time and harvest, the
reapers' song to the falling ears, his rejoicing when the
last load home is safely housed, invariably suggest

something deeper than an operation in agriculture to the cultivated mind. Since ever art first began to be, colour and ink have claimed a peculiar interest in browsing sheep and kine knee-deep in grass, and the men who tend them. But no other material has been so conventionalised as poor Hodge. He is seldom more than a mere figure in the landscape, as bereft of individuality as the cattleman with a forkful of hay on his shoulder, common in old prints of winter, or the bent old woman with a bundle of sticks, who is the perennial image of want. And the poet too thrusts this dim shape into his verse with a guess at his loves and griefs vaguer than his surmise of Philomel's sorrow, more random than his words for the laverock's music. As to novelists and playwrights, if they introduce a clown into their works at all, it is as a combination of all that is rude and stupid, an element in the rough contrasts of broad farce, a laughing-stock of the wits.

But Nature is superior to all poets and dramatists as a creator of character, and in the person of Robert Burns produced as if to shame them a rustic who if he had been a dream of Shakespeare's would have eclipsed every other portrait in his fancy's gallery. Before and since his time men have emerged from obscurity and want into the full light of fame, but the majority lose or hide their early characteristics as they move upward. Carlyle ascended by a plain though difficult path, at an early stage of which the outward marks of his village origin had changed into those of the philosopher and student. Earlier than Burns, his countryman Mallet, or rather Malloch, having attained to wealth and at least temporary fame, dissembled his lowly parentage and even his name. Both of these courses were impossible to Burns. Nature, as if her sole intent had been to display the poetry of toil, limited his experience to the one little patch of life that heretofore had been so imperfectly illuminated. She who 'ben i' the spence' had crowned him with 'polish'd leaves and berries red,' commanded that he was to paint 'the loves and ways of simple swains,' and was implicitly obeyed. From the day when he warbled his earliest rhyme to the 'puir hairst lassie,' who was his first partner on the corn-rigs, until his thirty-seventh year, when the black wings of death already overshadowed him, he sang the songs of rural labour.

One result has been to show that the common factor is larger, the peculiar possession smaller, in the various ranks of humanity than at first sight appears. It is a commonplace to say that the changes produced by wealth and luxury are more apparent than real. They do not prolong life, and it is doubtful if they add so very much to material enjoyment: for the ploughman's coarse bed of chaff is as soft to his strong limbs as his downy couch to the Sybarite; and the fragrant lord lover, though his lady be clad in silk and velvet, and his walk with her be under the boughs of his own gnarled oak and green chestnut-trees, can taste no deeper rapture of love than is felt by the gardener's lad who keeps the path tidy and at sundown meets his nutbrown maiden up the burnside where the ferns are and the heather grows. Nor does even prolonged study and intellectual cultivation produce any such mighty superiority as is sometimes assumed. Sir Walter said a wise word to Lockhart on the subject. 'I have,' he remarked, 'read books enough, and observed and conversed with enough of eminent and splendidly cultivated

minds; but I assure you I have heard higher sentiment
from the lips of poor, uneducated men and women . . .
than I ever met with out of the pages of the Bible.'
And after Carlyle had given more than man's allotted
span of life to thought and intellectual improvement
and literary labour, it was Burns who found a voice for
his tender regret, and he would often repeat the lines—

> 'Had we never loved sae kindly,
> Had we never loved sae blindly,
> Never met or never parted,
> We had ne'er been broken-hearted.'

Though the author of *Philip van Artevelde* was an
exception, nearly all the other cultured minds of the century, howsoever they differed in regard to others, have
agreed to think highly of Burns, who, in truth, is more
of a poet's poet than Spenser or Rossetti. Browning and
Swinburne united in loving him, as do Walt Whit-
man and Tennyson; Wordsworth and Coleridge and
Longfellow were among those who paid him 'the meed
of a melodious tear.' And the striking supplement
and contrast to this is the extraordinary and abiding
popularity of Burns among the men of his own class.
There is no other poet who, in the lowest grades of
society, is equally popular. Just as in his life-time his
talk had an equal fascination for high duchess and
humble ostler, so after a hundred years have passed
the rude unlettered peasant has as much delight in him
as the rich secluded scholar. The early wish that he
'some usefu' plan or beuk could make, or sing a sang
at least' has been amply fulfilled; for to his countrymen's ears the Bible itself is not more familiar than
Scots wha hae and *Should auld acquaintance* and *Willie
brew'd a peck o' maut*; many a ploughman and cottar

who hardly knows the name of Tennyson and never
reads a line of Shakespeare consoles himself with Robbie.
If 'the imagination that shudders at the hell of
Dante' is as Dante's own, then also this love and
appreciation of Burns is proof that the meanest drudge
who laughs at his *Tam o' Shanter* or is thrilled by his
songs is so far a poet like himself, and a living proof
that toil and poetry are not incompatible. The stiff
and strong-limbed drainer, who from dawn to dusk has
been monotonously heaving up oblongs of wet clay with
his long spade, is as likely to entertain passion and
tenderness and dream as a millionaire. The best verse
of Burns was not hummed in idleness to the running
brooks, but 'sowthed' at labour, like the tunes a merry
carpenter sings at his task ; and his was no light and
elegant exercise such as stimulates rather than deadens
mental energy, but the sordid, continuous toil that
behind it leaves weary limbs and aching bones. Reminiscences of physical exhaustion were always too
vivid and familiar for work to have in his eyes any of
the charm with which the moralist invests it. 'The
thresher's weary flingin'-tree the lee-lang day had tired
me,' he said, and left those who never handled a flail to
romance about the dignity of work ; when he triumphed
over its effects he did not prove that toil develops poetry,
only that it does not always destroy it. Unless gifted
with a spark of the same energy our typical labourer
will have his finer faculties cramped and atrophied
by spade-work, just as Darwin's appreciation of Shakespeare was destroyed by his devotion to material science,
or as the higher intellectual qualities of a millionaire
pine and wither from neglect while he is concentrating
his attention on stock exchange and market. And as

to that, there is no position in life so advantageous that
a man may not fall back from it into the beast, none so
bad it may not serve as stepping-stone to higher things
The uses to which men put wealth and the occupations
they find for leisure do not invariably inspire envy or
emulation.

Ease and Toil tend to produce quite opposite streams
of thought, each of which is, nevertheless, a supplement
rather than a contradiction of the other. Toil is deeply
concerned with the hard and immediate struggle for
existence; it hardly goes further than the aspiration—

> ' To make a happy fireside clime
>> For weans and wife,
>> That 's the true pathos and sublime
>> Of human life.'

But Ease has already accomplished this and is intent on
knowing what the next step shall be. It has time to
note how the irrevocable hours fly past and asks
whence and *whither*. In happy intervals Toil gladly
notes and sings the beauty of earth, Ease muses on its
meaning. One is bright and vigorous, the other soft
and melancholy. As an illustration of the difference
compare the burn in *Hallowe'en* with the brook of
Tennyson. How exquisite, how purely sensuous is the
description of Burns—

> ' Whyles owre a linn the burnie plays,
>> As thro' the glen it wimpl't :
>> Whyles round a rocky scar it strays :
>> Whyles in a wiel it dimpl't :
>> Whyles glitter'd to the nightly rays,
>> Wi' bickering, dancing dazzle ;
>> Whyles cookit underneath the braes,
>> Below the spreading hazel,
>>> Unseen that night.'

Burns has seen the picture as vividly as the other

and paints it with a finish and energy which no successor has rivalled. But though Lord Tennyson could not emulate the force of Burns, he could add something that was not within the Scottish poet's scope. With all the culture and dreams of his generation unconsciously and yet not dormant in his brain, he has walked musingly by the running water, and, the eternal problem facing him, even while searching words for its limpid music, has added the delicate note of melancholy and wonder that gives the inimitable tint to his canvas. Like that of Richard Jefferies, his brook flows on conscious yet careless of human change.

The thought is one that involuntarily saddens the contemplative student of Nature. 'I' while conscious am the centre of the universe and it is for me that the world goes round, but 'I' die and there is no change. The stars shine, the wind blows, the rain falls, and the little brook runs on 'for ever,' and the hills that at ruddy sunsets seemed to smile on me with peculiar intelligence look down on others with the same kindly mask of indifference. And the leisured student is not slow to discover also that the apparent beneficence of Nature is deceptive; for the system by means of which her operations are carried on is one of endless rapine. Life's tender sympathy with life undergoes continual outrage, for there is hardly an organism that is not nourished by murder; and, as if not content with stirring up deadly war among the fishes and beasts and birds and reptiles she has called into being, Nature at times in a rapture of causeless anger goes forth with her stormy artillery and kills and mangles and tortures till all but the dead lament. Yet Toil, because it is so engrossed in its individual battle, takes no account of

the general carnage, nor asks whether or not good is
indeed to be the final goal of ill. In despondent
moments of its bitter struggle for a poor foothold on
earth and the bare privilege of living it exclaims—

> 'O Death ! the poor man's dearest friend,
>   The kindest and the best !
> Welcome the hour my aged limbs
>   Are laid with thee at rest !
> The great, the wealthy fear thy blow,
>   From pomp and pleasure torn,
> But oh ! a blest relief to those
>   That weary laden mourn ! '

Ease, emancipated from the sordid struggle, bought
out as it were from this compulsory soldiering, may an'
it pleases make admiration the business of existence,
and by fresh rills, in pied meadows, lingering in green
dells, resting on brown mountain slopes, forget altogether
the wild dramas of life, or see only, as in a picture, its
' clanging fights, and flaming towns, and sinking ships,
and praying hands'; hear, but only as the still sad
music of a dream, the doleful song—

> 'Chanted from an ill-used race of men that cleave the soil,
> Sow the seed, and reap the harvest, with enduring toil
> Storing yearly little dues of wheat, and wine, and oil.'

The part Burns had to act in life was too intense
and difficult for him to forget the play in admiration of
the scenery; it was only in keen and hurried glances,
or in the too brief intervals between the acts, that he
marked how the drama was staged and set. Or as
Wordsworth put it, when expressing his surprise that
when he lived at Mossgiel or afterwards 'he never
adverted to the splendid prospects stretching towards
the sea and bounded by the peaks of Arran on one
part': 'It is as a human being, eminently sensitive

and intelligent, and not as a poet, clad in his priestly robes and carrying the ensigns of sacerdotal office, that he interests and affects us.' Burns himself much more clearly defined his position in a remark that has often been quoted. 'He once told me,' relates Dugald Stewart, 'when I was admiring a distant prospect in one of our morning walks, that the sight of so many smoking cottages gave a pleasure to his mind which none could understand who had not witnessed like himself their happiness and worth.' Poetry was not with him, as with Wordsworth, a musing over the significance of natural phenomena, but a re-living by dint of memory and imagination of the exquisitely painful or exquisitely happy hours of the past. The harvest moon shining on rigs of barley is glorified in fancy by association with Anna. Spring forgets to tell its message of hope to a bereaved lover—

> 'The snow-drop and primrose our woodlands adorn,
> And violets bathe in the weet o' the morn :
> They pain my sad bosom, sae sweetly they blaw,
> They mind me o' Nannie—my Nannie's awa.'

Bird and green brae and murmuring river take their cue from the poet, and are sober or gay of voice and mien in sympathy with him ; or a brilliant contrast is drawn if the season is wholly out of keeping with himself; his emotions never are guided nor he subdued by Nature. Her beautiful or desolate places are but staging for human comedy and tragedy ; her soft westlin' winds and wild tempestuous storms an orchestral accompaniment to action. It does not appear that he had any appetite for minute facts from the open air, such as we have seen Jefferies gather with delight ; or that his chief aim was 'to paint with Thomson's land-

scape glow'; or find sermons in stones, such as we
have had from Wordsworth and Mr. Ruskin. In his
art Nature is allotted the same incidental and sub-
sidiary part that Homer and Shakespeare and Milton
gave her.

To him, as to Pope, the greatest study of mankind
was man, and though many a bright epigram and
descriptive phrase showed a piercing judgment of
lawyers and statesmen and *literati*, his experience was
almost confined to the sons of toil. He is at home on
the harvest-field and the ploughland, in barn and stable
and stackyard, in lowly biggin' and wayside hostelry,
where 'drouthy neebors neebors meet'; his heroines
are milkmaids and serving-girls; their friends and
fathers and lovers are poor and frugal labourers. And
it is his chiefest glory to have shown those who are not
of this circle how 'one touch of Nature makes the whole
world kin'; how tears and laughter are the same
in cot and palace; how the hind in hodden grey loves
as rapturously as the laird, and the hamlet girl in her
poor gaiety of ribbons is as arch and coquettish as any
high-born damsel in laces and silk; that, as Teufels-
dröckh would have it, clothes make no essential difference in humanity.

And yet poverty has its own peculiar virtues. A
Scott or a Tennyson, a Shelley or a Byron, born into
that middle or upper class from which no subservience
is expected, has never felt the oppression that makes
a Burns fly for protection to Smollett's 'Lord of the
lion heart and eagle eye.' In what is called society
independence is properly enough taken for granted, and
the greatest loses nothing in dignity while he gains in
grace by cultivating a pleasing deference to others;

while he who stands too much on his dignity is use-
lessly boorish and aggressive, introducing as it were an
element of friction into the smooth and easy indifference
that is the crowning merit of social culture. Where
ordered intercourse is not only a chief pleasure but an
important business of life, it is necessary to observe the
unwritten laws that prevent the jar of a too assertive
individualism. The case stands very much otherwise
in the ranks to which Burns belonged.

In the first place indifference was to him an utterly
impossible virtue ; on the contrary he had not enough
of 'cautious, canny self-control' to guide his affairs
discreetly; and was brimming full of the emotions that
make life rich. Easy it is for most of us to jog lightly
and inoffensively through the world. He who drives a
team of full-blooded, unbroken thorough-breds runs
more risk of trouble than the applewoman with her
donkey. But Burns full of mirth uncontrollable ; and
wit and sarcasm as keen as his sense of humour ; and
tenderness that a flower—a mouse—a picture could
evoke ; and love unbounded and passion like a whirl-
wind ; how could he with steady features pace through
life like an automaton in a puppet show ? The eagerness and fervour with which these qualities were worn
made the owner of them peculiarly liable to feel the humi-
liations of poverty and to wince under its slights. And
withal there was something within him that reduced
to zero the authority—based upon the merely external
marks of circumstance—of those who fancied themselves
his superior, and induced him to retort with crushing
vigour. If some rigidly righteous elder of the kirk
rebuked his backslidings while Nature still consolingly
whispered that 'the light that led astray was light from

heaven,' he turned upon his tormentors and rent them with deadly satire. The Phariseeism of the false affected scholarship that was always offering to help him with pedantic patronising advice and formal rules he overturned as easily as Gareth did Death's grisly make-believe in the *Idylls*, and in winged words that still, wherever a show of learning attempts to beat down native intelligence by the mere braggadoccio of display, are as deadly as ever—

> ' A set o' dull, conceited hashes
> Confuse their brains in college classes,
> They gang in stirks and come oot asses,
>   Plain truth to speak ;
> An' syne they think to climb Parnassus
>   By dint o' Greek.'

As a matter of fact no other poet has risen as high as Burns with so slender an equipment, and he would be a foolish aspirant who made the verse an excuse to despise learning, yet it is a well-merited rebuke of those who, without any high intellectual gift, dub themselves critics because they know something of particles and prosody. I quote it here as an example of the independence that, mine where you will, is discovered as the bedrock of the character of Burns. For him, as for Carlyle, the only aristocracy was that of mind and character, and 'the birkie ca'ed a laird' without these had no title to respect. 'The noble Glencairn,' he wrote in his Edinburgh diary, 'has wounded me to the soul here, because I dearly esteem, respect, and love him. He showed so much attention, engrossing attention, one day to the only blockhead at table (the whole company consisted of his lordship, dunder-pate, and myself) that I was within half a point of throwing down my gage of contemptuous defiance.' It is the 'man of abilities,

his heart glowing with honest pride,' who is galled and
hurt by conventional deference to the false show made
by wealth. National independence carried straight
to the heart of his countrymen the words of the
triumphantly assertive song—

> ' The rank is but the guinea's stamp
> The man's the gowd for a' that.'

It is easy to forgive the tone of almost reckless defiance
with which the poet praises a virtue that the circumstances of toil tend to wither and destroy, for few labouring men have strength of mind to see ' an independency
at the plough tail ' or consolation in reflecting that
' the last o't, the warst o't, is only for to beg '; to few
is it given to understand how evenly after all happiness
is distributed, and what a small fraction is at the mercy
of fortune. To the great majority, for example, it seems
only a pleasant freak of the imagination to show as
Burns does ' a merry crew of randie, gangrel bodies,'
enjoying themselves with a rapture kings might envy.
Towsie drab and merry-andrew, tinker, common thief,
soldier, and wandering fiddler, selling their last rags to
keep the fun going, mocking the cheated world and
making the rafters ring with their merriment of
laughter and song—where in literature is there anything like it, where in life such another satire upon the
happiness to be bought with money ? Independence of
title, treasure, and even reputation itself, is no small
part of the poetry of toil.

One clear advantage of being born to humble circumstances is that it supplies a definite purpose to life
from the outset. A child of ease, whose forefathers by
industry or good luck have redeemed him from the
curse of labour, is apt to drift aimlessly in search of a

task or a mission, and ere he finds either is blown upon by so many relaxing winds of doctrine he thinks no port worth making for. If he eventually fasten to a pursuit, he becomes either a mere dabbler, or an inherited love of work causes him to labour as if he were himself a child of toil, and he volunteers for the service he was emancipated from. But the poor man is under the same compulsion that makes the wild beast hunt for his prey, the wild bird forage for his food ere he carols from the spray; the continuation of the life with which he has been dowered is dependent on his capacity to gather support for it; his first and imperative mission being to earn a livelihood, he does not suffer from any lack of purpose. The contract between him and Nature is sternly hard and clear; he rents the right to exist by a daily payment of labour, and probably in its harshest form feels the pressure of Nature's command that life cannot be save where there is exertion. If he does not now roam the thicket and the wood, gathering wild berries on the hillside and nuts by the windy coppice, he has to assist in finding food by methods that are only a little more complicated. But no labour is so constant and severe as to be wholly destitute of breaks and interludes, wherein joy is rendered all the more intense by the very force of contrast; and in these interludes 'the wild joy of living' flashes with intense brilliance upon those fortunate individuals who share the quality of forgetfulness.

Pleasure is a deity who will not be propitiated by the richness and pomp of her votaries. Although it is customary to allude to Burns in terms of pity, and talk as though his life had been utterly miserable and wasted, it is doubtful if ever there was accorded to another man so many hours of rapt and ecstatic happiness. Yet he was utterly divorced from pursuits that are the delight of ease and culture. Books were not to him the solace they were to Carlyle, the cotter's son had not Scott's early training to sport, gambling with its excitement had no place in his sphere, want of education stood in the way of scientific amusements such as Goethe loved, the fine arts were closed to him, and his means permitted but little indulgence in the luxuries of dress, travel, or food. Poverty, that tethers a man to a single spot of ground and loads him with care, also rears a high wall between him and the beautiful refinement of life. In compensation she learns him to love and to laugh with a force and abandon unknown to the delicate melancholy that flows at length from the prolonged broodings of culture, the growing and unappeasable appetite of wealth. With a sun-tanned harvest girl, or a dishevelled dairy maid, at the kitchen table beside a haggis, in a tavern over 'reaming swats that drank divinely,' he quaffed full deep draughts of the pleasures of earth, and though (to continue the simile) the cup was homely as the horn from which ploughmen drink their ale, the wine was pure, and of the same old vintage that inspired the songs of Sappho and Anacreon, of Ovid and Catullus, and all the bards who have a place in England's Helicon. For the poetry of love depends neither on rich drapery nor pink complexion, but on the fancy and ardour of the lover; just as the poetry of eating and drinking arises from capacity for enjoyment, not from the connoisseur's fastidious tastes. In this country, where wine always has been practically confined to the rich, its praises never have been sung so well as those of nut-brown ale and 'barley bree.'

It is not to be imagined that because Burns was an exceptionally gifted member of the class to which he belonged that he expressed sentiments and perceptions unnatural to toil. On the contrary, the manner in which his verse has passed into the common everyday speech of Scottish ploughmen affords proof that he interpreted their feelings when he expressed his own. No doubt a very plausible case might be made out to show that the preference of this class is rather than not a condemnation of literature. In the songs that attain a sudden currency and popularity among them, a rude smartness passes for wit, and the pathos seems childishly foolish and sentimental. But these faults are strictly analogous to those found in the drawing-room ditty that is fashionable one season and forgotten the next; for the immediate judgment of no class of society is of much value. For a hundred years now successive generations have returned again and again to his verse, as mankind does only to that which is immortal.

In a highly cultivated age the natural tendency of poets is to write for a select few rather than the general, and many who are esteemed among the greatest of the century are practically unknown to the average citizen. To take but a few names, Shelley and Rossetti, Browning and Matthew Arnold and Mr. Swinburne, if they would not take it as an insult to be understood and recited by the unlettered, at all events did not dream of addressing a portion of the public to which their dialect is Greek. But it is worthy of note that a far other ambition inspired that small body of

verse that has proved its claim to immortality. The
great epic of Greece was composed for the ear of
warriors and not for the closet; Shakespeare and
Molière wrote primarily to seize the attention of
miscellaneous audiences from the theatre; even Dante
indited his 'mystic unfathomable song' with an eye to
the common folk. While learned poets, whose books
were dedicated to the greatest men of the time, such,
for example, as Ammonius, the friend of Erasmus, pass
entirely out of knowledge, the ballad composed by some
nameless bard to amuse shepherd and ploughman is
kept in memory by successive generations of old
women crooning it at the spinning wheel or telling it
to children; and at last it is enshrined as an ornament
to literature. So too with compositions like the Lied
of the Niebelungen, and that immortal song of 'Roland
brave and Olivier' chanted by Taillefer, as he advanced
a willing sacrifice to omen at the battle of Senlac; they
were made for the express purpose of being easily
apprehended by the uneducated understanding. The
modern author assumes that to appreciate poetry a
special training is necessary, and he writes for those
who have obtained it, with the very common result that
his meaning becomes so overlaid with affectations and
artificialities, so wrapped up in the pomp of trope and
verbiage, that it has entirely lost any power it may
have originally possessed to touch the simple natural
passions of man.

At the very best, language is an imperfect medium
for holding intercourse between mind and mind.
Neither in paint nor in music nor in words is the most
consummate artist able to do more than faintly adum-
brate his mental impressions; the fine glories of bright

joy that pass in fitful transient flashes, the vivid
sensuous pleasures that come only in moments when
life is at the flood, and the soul almost supernaturally
awake, the longing and sorrow, the despair and hope of
which existence is compact almost elude expression.
And indeed the minor poet attempts no more than to
flutter gracefully around his idea, using it may be forms
as dainty as those of a Ronsard, weaving lines musical
as those of Poe, choosing words as lovingly as a Herrick.
Nor are his efforts by any means to be despised. Is there
any singer of the present day deserving of neglect? By
no means one among the score or so who are dubbed
men of genius in contemporary biography. Yet we
know very well from experience of the past that the
age would be fortunate if it possessed one truly great.
Not once in a century, not more than once in many
centuries is an immortal born. The reign of Elizabeth
was more prolific of literary talent than that of Victoria,
yet of that 'nest of singing birds' one only has stoutly
withstood the ravages of time. Ben Jonson and
Webster, Marlowe and Greene, and Beaumont and
Fletcher are still no doubt read and loved by some of
us, but Shakespeare alone remains a vital force in
English literature; and of all that he wrote nothing is
more securely fixed in public estimation than simple
verses like the dirge in *Cymbeline* dealing with
primal and elemental truths about the life of man.
The example is chosen, not because it is the most
excellent passage in Shakespeare, but forasmuch as it has
a particular application to the toiling race of man—

> 'Fear no more the heat o' the sun,
> Nor the furious winter's rages,
> Thou thy worldly task hast done,
> Home hast gone, and ta'en thy wages.'

Now Burns more than any other modern wrote for the express purpose of catching the ear of toil. The audience he thought of was composed of Ayrshire peasants, and he addressed them in terms as natural and direct as ever were employed by the homeliest ballad-maker. He had no wide choice of form. Robert Fergusson, the unfortunate poet—who was his favourite model, and whose tragical death on a straw pallet in Edinburgh workhouse at the age of twenty-four occurred when his Ayrshire successor was a boy of fifteen— had been, though a dissipated, a gentle and scholarly poet, but in his Scottish verse had followed the metres of Allan Ramsay and those who had gone before him. A comparison between *Hallowfair* and *Hallowe'en*, or between *The Farmer's Ingle* and the *Cotter's Saturday Night*, to say nothing of others, shows how clearly the disciple followed a master he was soon to surpass. It could not escape the shrewd eye of Burns, however, that Fergusson had always been most successful when treating humble themes in the dialect of the street and the tavern. There is not one of his English pieces worth preserving for its own sake, and gleanings from the classics—echoes of Horace and adaptations of Virgil, with all the *dramatis personæ* of ancient mythology— that have served the turn of so many rhymesters (and prosemen too for the matter of that) added nothing to the beauty or force of his expression. In one respect this was fortunate. Burns, who never could exist out of his own element, who could not hymn a strange river, nor describe a scene till he had lived with it, nor make himself at home in school English, never could have mastered Lemprière with the facility of a Keats. If he could not write in his own tongue to his own folk,

and on the simple themes suggested by rustic life, it
was useless for him to attempt doing so at all.'

The peasants for whom he wrote would only have
been perplexed by his adoption of a complicated poetic
machinery; and very few of the heathen gods and
goddesses, such as Apollo and Venus and Cupid, were
known to them except by name. Nevertheless in their
thrift and industry, the ardour of their enthusiasms and
their intervals of gaiety, the strength of their domestic
virtues and the warmth of their loves and hates they
represented labour at its highest. There were Holy
Willies and Dr. Hornbooks and Unco Guids among
them in abundance, but there were also those who
delighted to strip the mask from hypocrisy and make a
laughing-stock of the quack, and mock at the extreme
Puritan. With the majority, however, the struggle for
existence was so hard and inveterate that everything
unessential was worn away from life, and it was idle to
address to them any literature that dealt with feigned
regret or spurious hopes or artificial raptures. Up to
then the poetry for which they had showed esteem was
that in which the vicissitudes of life are dealt with
truthfully, vigorously, and sternly. Bookshelves that
might be otherwise empty were certain to contain at
least a Bible, and the ordinary talk of ploughmen
explained how it was that the Psalms of David and
the Book of Job were portions the most thumbed. At
the ingle they would pass hours in recitation of *Clerk
Saunders* and *Sir Patrick Spens* and other ballads:
they forgathered at the wayside clachan to sing old
songs, in which ribald fun and filth were grotesquely
intermingled with exquisite pathos and pure humour.

But the great and important fact in all their lives

was the sore labour with which they were vexed. And
if the bard of Coila has, in showing them the bright
gleams playing about that hard lot, interpreted far
wider emotions, it is largely on account of the fact that
upon all of us the primitive curse still rests. If toil be
substituted for war, it will be found that a striking
analogy exists between the first audience of Burns and
that of Homer. Equally simple and illiterate, they
were interested in literature only so far as it reflected
the stirring episodes, passions, and events of life.

A great critic has said of Wordsworth that hardly
any one has tried to praise him without praising him
well; the exact opposite is true of Burns. Of the
many who have written his biography none has succeeded in adding a classic to our language. From
Chambers and Lockhart to Shairp and Blackie each
has produced a book more or less ineffectual and unsatisfactory. With the exception of Carlyle and (more
doubtfully) of Mr. Louis Stevenson, the essayists have
been equally unable to account for a bard so rude and
unlettered having been able to 'capture the hearts of a
whole people' as Mr. Andrew Lang admits he did; and
Mr. Lang is one of the few Scotsmen who love him
not. But the same pleasant essayist allows to him
'the large utterance of the early hinds,' finds his love-
poems unexcelled by Catullus, and places him beside
Theocritus as a rural bard. Matthew Arnold too,
despite the appreciation of his master—Goethe—was
inclined to 'lightly' him. It could not well be otherwise. We live in an age of extreme cultivation, of
microscopic research, and minute analysis; our favourite
poetry reflects 'the questions of the day' and 'the
spirit of the age'; in verse are discussed the doubts

fears, hopes, beliefs, and unbeliefs of a sceptical generation.   Of these ideas the mind of the student of literature is full, and in Burns he finds neither help nor
guidance.   He desires something to feed a delicate
melancholy, and he is given an uproarious drinking
chorus: he asks if life is worth living, and he is
answered with a love-song; he searches for some subtle
refinement of joy or sorrow, and he comes upon a hymn
in praise of haggis.   If there is lamentation, it is no
chant of subtle, pensive sadness, but a cry of grief as
piercing and natural as the moan of a dying wild beast.
The rejoicing has no sober tinge or background, the
lover and the reveller burst into melody without
analysing the cause of bliss.   So it happens that the
critic of to-day, whose mind is an echoing cavern for a
million distracting cries, finds in Burns neither solace
nor enjoyment.   Fronting the great mystery of existence here is a fiddling Nero, singing and laughing and
weeping over all the sordid trivial struggles that to him
who is facing Eternity have such slight importance.
And they raise their hands in wonder at a popularity
that they can only explain by the rustic ignorance of
his admirers.

Ah yes, but the great poets who have lived since the
death of Burns—the greatest of them the most enthusi-
astically—have loved their ploughman brother as
ardently as any Ayrshire hind or Scots day labourer.
To Sir Walter and Carlyle and Tennyson it has been
revealed that life as sung by Burns is life indeed, that
joy and change and death are, save for a few insignificant details, the same in the cottage as in the palace,
and that whosoever has thrilled the heart of one honest
man with his verse may thrill the whole world, and

that the Laureate of toil is the Laureate of the human race. It is but the lady's maid who loves to see the characters of fiction betitled; to him who truly knows men and books, even there 'the rank is but the guinea's stamp,' and the labourer is as interesting as the lord.

Nay more, is it not apparent that here at any rate the voice of the people is the voice of God? Mad and foolish as its first loud clamour usually is, as the years flow by the muddied stream of opinion grows clear and beautiful. And in our time the popular verdict, that it is the fashion of superfine critics to jeer at, has an authority greater than it ever had before. The author who among the millions of readers craving for suitable mental food is not able to conquer one small territory, is not able to gather to himself a following, is most likely unworthy of one. But he who like Burns satisfies generation after generation, whose verse is a household word, and whose lines are quoted like proverbs or texts from Holy Writ, is assured of his place. To speak of his work as the poetry of toil is perhaps a pleonasm. He was a labourer it is true; so are we all. The life that pulsates in every line, the force, the humour, the pathos, and the scorn of the man echo where weariness has no association with the furrowed field.

VII

THE DIVINITY OF NATURE

(WORDSWORTH)

No sooner do the ablest and most appreciative of the critics of Wordsworth's poetry come to his religion than they become sternly logical and prosaically matter-of-fact. If 'our birth is but a sleep and a forgetting,' what is it that we have forgotten?—if 'trailing clouds of glory do we come,' where are those clouds? are their strict and mechanical tests. And the result is that even admirers of the poet as hearty as the late Matthew Arnold or Mr. John Morley dismiss the doctrine as having 'no real solidity.' When he says 'Heaven lies about us in our infancy,' they attach no more import-ance to the *dictum* than they would to a doting mother's belief, that when a smile dimples the waxen cheek of her sleeping babe it is dreaming of a Paradise where before it was playmate to angels. As after a stormy voyage by sea the inn bed seems to heave and rock as if riding on billows, so the hunting dog still chases in his sleep,and from under the child's eyelid come tears, or its lips wreathe into a smile as the shadows of its little joys and sorrows return and haunt the brain.

In like manner the cold light of reason is thrown on other points of the Wordsworthian creed, as, for example, the inspired vision of childhood that gradually wanes

with the years till 'the things which I have seen I now
can see no more.' With this idea Matthew Arnold had
no sympathy whatever, and called in the aid of Thucy-
dides to cover it with gentle raillery. Nevertheless it
needs no prolonged study of Nature's most eloquent
lovers to show that the poet was standing on firmer
ground than his critic admits. 'The instinct of delight
in Nature and her beauty had no doubt extraordinary
strength in Wordsworth himself as a child. But to say
that universally this instinct is mighty in childhood,
and tends to die away afterwards, is to say what is
extremely doubtful. In many people, perhaps with the
majority of educated persons, the love of Nature is
nearly imperceptible at ten years old, but strong and
operative at thirty.' But will this opinion of Mr.
Arnold's hold true of the typical lovers of Nature whose
lives we have been considering? Carlyle was just ten
on 'the red sunny Whitsuntide morning' when he
went to Annan Grammar School, and the phrase we
have quoted from _Sartor_ is proof that his perceptions
were keen enough at this early age. Lord Tennyson at
eighty is still haunted by memories of the scenery of
his childhood, nor has he given us any picture drawn
from the experience of his middle or later life so
graphic and perfect as one or two of the phrases in
which for all time he has portrayed the Lincolnshire
fields wherein he played as a boy. Among the last
sentences dictated by Richard Jefferies were those
recalling the drifting crowds, the sparkling water at
Coate when as a child he watched the barred pike in
the brook. Thoreau learned to love Walden in wanderings that almost belonged to infancy; Burns never wrote
so well of other streams as he did of the Nith, the Ayr,

and the Lugar; and of Jefferies, Thoreau, and Burns
the work was all done before the first borderland of old
age was reached.   It was in the early years spent at
Sandyknowe that Sir Walter learned to love the
Borderland, and we have many proofs in his verse that
he delighted to linger over his infantile memories.
Not only so, but the study of almost any poet's childhood, in connection with his works, will show that his
strongest, most vivid, and most lasting impressions of
Nature were his earliest.

So far therefore it is Wordsworth and not his critic
who is right. The 'instinct of delight,' not only in
Nature, but in everything, is stronger at ten—ten with
its fresh pure innocence—than ever it can possibly be
to the mature and critical soberness of thirty; for delight
does not necessarily increase with experience and the
ripening of taste, but prefers quick young blood and
exuberant life, and hope that still is sanguine, and a past
that does not yet cast shadows on the present.   What
supreme comedian will ever evoke such a transport of
merriment as the first rude pantomime produced?
What triumph of 'victorious middle-age' yields a
pleasure equal to what was derived from the first gun
or angle? And so likewise there is no sun of after-
life more bright and kindly than that which shone
on school holidays; conservatories produce no flowers
equal in tint to the weeds we then picked by the wayside; and birds sang and chirped with a melody and
eloquence when we idly roved the field for their nests
that still are unsurpassed. And the delight was not
less from being accepted unconsciously. To formulate
one's likings and dislikings, to criticise, to select, and to
become fastidious are results of the culture that puri-

fies taste but adds no jot or iota to the intensity of enjoyment. Sensuous pleasure gratifies the sense that is open and virgin to it with a fulness that passes away as sense grows satiate and jaded. But this fact, that overturns the opinion of Mr. Arnold, proves no more about Wordsworth than that he was correct in his perception. It does not follow that he was correct in his inference, that the exquisite pleasure arises from a Divine effluence lingering about youth till it is gradually put to flight as

> ' Shades of the prison-house begin to close
> Upon the growing boy.'

But it leaves it still as an open question whether the most famous stanza in Wordsworth's most famous ode did really express a glimmering of truth, or is only a pretty and sentimental fancy. And one might go through all his poems in the same way in hesitating search of a label for the author's opinions. It were, however, as unprofitable to ask whether he was at bottom Pagan or Pantheist or Christian as it is to argue about his style or the exact place he should hold in a class list of English poets.

If Wordsworth is pleasant to read it is on account neither of his direct religious and moral teaching, nor by reason of his expression, but because he has like no other entered deeply into the joy of earth. Indeed the very odour of newly dug soil seems to hang about his verse; when most dull and tiresome he suggests at worst the weariness of a long journey over a dull landscape. At his best the charm he wields is comparable only to that of sunlight on waving corn, of birds singing on flowery hawthorn, of the brook chattering round its ferny islets.

M

Nevertheless, the young generation, that accepts the doctrine of evolution as implicitly as Christianity used to be accepted, is likely in a high degree to share in that distrust of the poet's optimism formulated by Mr. Morley. Can we or can we not sympathise with the jubilant ecstasy of such lines as these?—

> 'I hear the echoes through the mountains throng,
>   The winds come to me from the fields of sleep,
>   And all the earth is gay ;
>   Land and sea
>   Give themselves up to jollity
>   And with the heart of May
>   Doth every beast keep holiday ;—
>   Thou Child of Joy,
>   Shout round me, let me hear thy shouts, thou happy Shepherd boy.'

And he proceeds to discover that the heavens laugh with the blessed creatures in their jubilee and 'the fulness of your bliss, I feel—I feel it all.' Surely 'the wild joy of living' has here reached its culminating expression.

To the sober, and perhaps slightly cynical, *fin de siècle* reader the ecstasy seems to result from a somewhat superficial view of the earthly paradise whereof it was written. Even on a May morning Nature does not realise the promise that 'they shall not hurt nor destroy in all my holy mountain, saith the Lord.' At the best all this flaunting glory of leaf and blossom is a vain and transitory apparition, an automatic show depending on temperature. The cold dead wilderness of winter blossoms like the rose as soon as the mercury rises. Nature that begot this profusion of life will reduce it again with reckless cruelty. Ruthlessly will she wither and destroy all those lusty striving plants, and she will not only kill but, purposelessly as far as we can see,

starve and torture millions of the apparently happy
creatures. As if that were not enough, she has im-
planted a murderous enmity between life and life, and
the 'blessed creatures' find 'the fulness of their bliss'
in war and bloodshed. The dimple that shows so
limpidly on the shining stream tells of a salmon rising
at a fly or chasing the minnows, in haste to kill something, just as the angler and the otter are intent in
their turn on its destruction. And the birds that lend
such an exquisite charm to the summer landscape are
nearly all bent on rapine. It is not only that the merlin
and the kestrel swoop down on thrush and linnet, but
the birds most loved by the poet, those most frequently
used to symbolise peace and gentleness, the legendary
robin, the swallow, 'chasing itself at its own wild will,'
are equally bound on the same fell errand. By the
roadside clump of nettles, or under the patches of blue
speedwell, the weasel is feasting on the wren, the
rat slaying the mouse. On the desolate St. Paul's
Rocks, where there were no other inhabitants, Darwin
found the grapsus at war with the noddy, the tern
feasting on the flying-fish. Nature is no bountiful and
kindly mother feeding and guarding her offspring, but
to be personified as the evil and malignant mistress of
infinite millions of warring and discordant lives. There
are bloodstains on all her palace gates. In green bower
and leaf-curtained copse, in the pure atmosphere that
divides the blue sky from ploughland and cornfield,
under heaving exquisite seas that smile to the sunshine,
in silvery brooks that ripple through the land and
across the dusty highways, on bleak moor and fertile
garden, in lake and mountain and forest, the one constant spectacle is that of murderous tyranny and
oppression, that of the strong killing and devouring the

weak. Beast and bird, fish and snake and insect—
this is their chief occupation.

Nor is there discernible in Nature any beneficent
care of man. The rain falls alike on the evil and the
good. Who sets out on an errand of pity is as much
at the mercy of billow and thunderbolt, of fog and frost
and snow as the prowling thief and assassin. Disease
and affliction come upon the righteous man as frequently as upon the unrighteous. 'Nature never did
betray the heart that loved her' says the poet, but the
story of her lovers is the saddest on record. We have
seen how Thoreau worshipped her, and ruled his conduct by her precepts, and how he was rewarded with a
crown of sorrow and an early death. His fate was
enviable compared to that of Richard Jefferies. The
return for his adoration, accompanied though it was by
a fine innocent abstemiousness and frugality, was pain
and famine heaped upon him as by some bitter unre-
lenting fiend. Were it not that Nature habitually acts
traitor to her lovers, the saying 'whom the Gods love
die young' never would have passed into a proverb.
Yet after all, her attitude is not that of hate but
of indifference. Whether the wind come laden with
health or carrying the germs of disease it croons the
same meaningless tune to the pollards and the oak. On
harvest- and battle-field, on dead wrecked sailor and
prosperous merchantman, the moon dreamily rains its
beams. And in winter, when all the mute creation is
dying of cold and hunger, Nature clothes the earth with
a beauty unrivalled by summer. Upon the grey-
wooded hill-sides, upon snow-wreaths worked by the
sportive winds, upon plantations set in a dusky halo,
upon wide white fields and rivers black by contrast, the
wintry sun looks calmly down.

At bottom it is this pessimistic view of Nature that accounts for the melancholy that for a long time has been stealing across the face of literature as a mist gradually enwraps a Highland Ben. By the new cosmogony life's dignity and importance have been reduced to something infinitely less than

'A turmoil of ants in the gleam of a million million of suns.'

In a plague-stricken mediæval town, while the superstitious clothed themselves in sackcloth and chanted the *Miserere*, others more reckless and defiant went to the opposite extreme, and in wine and wassail, in mad wild merriment and debauchery, chased the hours till their turn came and death beckoned the revellers away. A somewhat similar picture is visible just now when, not only scrofulous French novelists and poets give themselves to the invention of a new moan that will match Baudelaire's shudder, but the most philosophic of Continental as well as of English novelists delight in planning a plot that will either make suicide inevitable or enable the curtain to be rung down on an array of blasted and hopeless lives ; and in sharp contrast with this madness of sorrow there is a school of non-moralists, who not only act on but vigorously preach as gospel the doctrine of the fool, ' Let us eat, drink, and be merry to-day, for to-morrow we die.' And it is hardly credible that the new joy invented by Wordsworth (according to Mr. Myers) can be a message of glad tidings to either of them.

The ghost of Achilles declared it better to be the thrall of a landless man than bear sway over all the kingdoms of the dead, and whatever life may be, the one universal truth about it is, that it is the dearest treasure in our possession, one that brings with it a watchful, guarding, striving instinct. Human existence is but a long endeavour to keep the flame alight, and no one who is greatly to be trusted has pictured it as more than a dreary watch relieved by fitful gleams of pleasure. Our greatest teacher was a man of sorrow, and the most philosophic of modern minds returned by Pagan ways to a doctrine of renunciation. In Shakespeare's mind life resolved itself into 'a tale told by an idiot,' and Dante's taste of its bitterness enabled him to picture the tortures of hell. Scott dealt out bliss with a royal hand to the world of his imagination, but, as if to dispel the effect of his dreams, chronicled his own misery in a journal that is sadder than Carlyle's. And where there has been no extraordinary misfortune such as his, and no strong passion, and no turbulent, self-torturing ambition, you shall still discover in the most serene and tranquil life an ineffable sadness. Look for example at Edward Fitzgerald. Was there ever man more amiable in character, more fortunate in his friends, more lovable, more beloved? And yet to read through his letters, which naturally and unintentionally reflect youth's eager brightness and the shadows that gathering in middle age deepen to its close, is to feel a sadness deeper than Hamlet's. And almost any truthful diary tells the same story of pain, grief, and ultimate loneliness when early friends have 'one by one crept silently to rest.' Life is perhaps not quite so gloomy as *The Mill on the Floss*, or so disappointing as it was to Risler aîné, but its sky is never quite clear, and we have reason to be glad if the clouds have but a tinge of brightness. Nor is the gay non-moralist able to rebel with effect against the general doom. From Catullus down to Mr.

Swinburne and Paul Verlaine, the singers of untrammelled joy have drifted into melancholy despite themselves, whenever they came into full view of 'Time with a gift of tears, grief with a glass that ran.'

Thus in opposition to Wordsworth we have founders of religion who, feeling the groaning and travail of creation, have tried to brighten the dolour of earth with a hope and vision of heaven; we have close students and lovers of life driven despite themselves to the conclusion that 'man was made to mourn'; scientific observers who note that the external world is the scene of pitiless cruelties—an arena of ceaseless war and bloodshed among the lower animals, a place where the profusion with which life is multiplied is equalled only by the ruthlessness with which it is swept back again into oblivion; and we have the further fact that man cannot if he would eat, drink, and be merry at his fill. The vicissitudes and calamities of life—disease and death and evil fortune—lie in wait to throttle his gladness and laughter, and despite his intent the joyous carol changes into a lament, and the merry jest to a sigh. Even Wordsworth himself declined from his midday splendour. After middle life 'the light that never was on sea or land' faded from his eyesight. 'It is no exaggeration to say,' remarks Matthew Arnold, 'that within one single decade . . . between 1798 and 1808 almost all his really first-rate work was produced.' And he was born in 1770.

But if he took a view too sanguine of the world's blessedness, they are no less in error who have wailed over its impenetrable gloom. At the heart of man there is something of Nature's own indifference, so that it is surprising how little his cheerfulness is impaired by crowding disaster. The bird that when its mate is killed will not have another by sunset, but will mourn its loss, is a rare exception to the general rule. Wild creatures seem to know nothing of regret or remorse, and only the first rudiments of sorrow. Joy and terror and care come to their existence as erratically as clouds and sunshine to our English sky; passing and leaving no deeper impression than the shadows that flicker in an English landscape. A bird after narrowly escaping the gunshot that has laid its companions dead flies to a safe distance, and soon begins unconcernedly to eat again; the fish that manages to wriggle off the hook and escape just as the angler is landing him, weary and wounded though he be, will not unfrequently accept the same bait offered once more by the same hand. Man's higher organisation is more sensitive; and yet when stripped of all his unreal and conventional and pretended sorrows he shares this animal instinct in a high degree. For a moment he may rebel against what he according to his creed calls the hand of fate, or the decrees of Providence, or the operations of Nature; but ultimately the healthy mind feeling itself to be part and parcel of a greater machinery submissively exclaims (in a dialect fashioned by belief), 'The Lord giveth and the Lord taketh away; Blessed be the name of the Lord.' Indeed it is utterly impossible for man to carry on any but a feigned and unnatural or more or less insane rebellion against destiny or the dispensation of Providence. Things, to brood on which would lead to madness, are forgotten with the lapse of time, and our capacity to sympathise with the sufferings of others is strictly limited. Even a humane man is interested rather than grieved to see an owl pounce on a frisky young rabbit, and he would indeed be a sentimentalist who shed tears for the thrushes found dead after a snow-storm. These occurrences are due to laws of Nature over which we have no control, and therefore give rise to mourning that is artificial only.

Men have ingeniously invented doctrines to justify a hardness of heart that shocks them. What the heathen philosophers called stoicism, in the vocabulary of a gentler creed became Christian resignation ; the Turk's 'kismet' is but a different version of the Presbyterian Scot's doctrine of predestination. In conversing with very aged men I have often thought the temperament most conducive to length of days, and therefore most in accordance with Nature, was a benevolent coldness, such as is exemplified in characters so different as those of Wellington and Goethe. It is to the hot passionate minds of their opposites that we owe so many contrivances to secure forgetfulness; as the Chinaman realises heaven in a dream, or a poet drowns sorrow in wine, or the Mahometan fronts death braced like the martyr with a hope of Paradise. The materialist, who will have it that every little handful of dust that we call living, every pigeon and cony and man and horse and dog is but a device of force escaping from earth and therefore as much subject to the control of law—as rigidly conditioned—as clouds driven by the wind, as water playing in a fountain ; that, in a word, all the fantastic tricks played by man, his romantic love-makings and wild adventures, his goings-out and comings-in, his strange feats with this and the other contrivance, his so-called subdual of wave and thundercloud, as well as his deep musings and high visions, his religions and literature, his art and his aspirations, are strictly auto-

matic, inevitable effects of causes beyond his control—
he who advances this is only a fatalist in a new guise.
He has returned to the belief that the world is no
random accident, but is guided and sustained by a Being
of infinite power. To him at least there is nothing
surprising in the doctrine that the lily rejoices in its
own loveliness, and the forest trees actually mourn when
rude November winds strip them of their glorious
raiment. To him, as to Carlyle, the natural and the
supernatural are one, and the universe is the vesture of
God.

But no man in the innermost depths of despair
wholly believes himself an automaton. Experience has
shown that to a considerable extent he is master of his
fate. Often he drifts into a haven for which he sets no
sail, often he feels himself guided when he fain would
have held the rudder, often with Shakespeare he is forced
to exclaim 'there's a divinity that shapes our ends,
rough-hew them how we will,' but nevertheless circumstance is not rigid but plastic. Effort is invariably
crowned with some measure of success, and with man
always rests a choice as to whether he will yield or do
battle. As a grey stone sent bounding down a green
ferny hill resembles in its leap from tussock to tussock
the hurried scamper of a rabbit, but is nevertheless
guided in every jump and spring by the character of
the ground, while the living creature may stay and turn
according to its own impulses, so does the automatic
man of theory differ from the actually real man.

Yet the analogy with Nature is not destroyed.
Force may, as has been thought, be at root uniform, so
that the energy with which I love and think be but a
driblet from that which makes the distant planet whirl

in his circle, but its manifestations are in continual conflict. The clouds do not always drift across heaven in orderly procession, but sometimes advance against each other like opposing armies; with a clash and a roar wind and wave in mad battle fling themselves on the rock, and life lives in unending strife with life.

Men like Thoreau, who set themselves to live in close accordance and adjustment with Nature, thereby assert their belief in the possession of a will beyond her influence as implying that at their choice they might withstand her behests; and this were incredible on the assumption that we are an integral part of her. She, for instance, tells us that self-preservation is her first law, and when storm and tempest arise her command is for us to fly to shelter, for her children keep an unrelaxed vigil against the approach of death. Yet it is not uncommon for a compassionate man, hoping for no gain or reward, to emerge from his stronghold, carrying as it were his life in his hand ready to yield it for the succour of others. Nor is life prized so very extravagantly that where there is a chance of gain men will not gamble with it, risking its loss in the hope of winning means for deeper enjoyment. The soldier for a paltry sum of money and the rations of a year or two will cheerfully allow himself to be shot. Life is a treasure at our free disposal to hoard or to spill or to waste. As the creature advances and develops he grows to be less at the mercy of Nature's malignance. He protects himself against the chill frost that annually lays flower and insect dead in millions; he learns to escape the thunderbolt, the tempest, and the snowdrift; he even curbs the murderous tendency in his own blood, till bloodshed that is every day in a state of Nature

becomes with him a rare horror and wonderment.
Independence of Nature changes into arrogance, and
behind urban fortifications he loses admiration of green
hill and blue sky, hardly attends to the unending
change of the seasons, and is defiant of the very fogs
that hide the shining of the stars. But his premature
endeavour to break the chains of his thraldom to earth
cause him to incur severe chastisement. With the ant
that stores its little hoard of grain, the bee that fills her
cells with honey, the squirrel who houses a harvest of
nuts he shares a desire to provide against famine that
he feeds till it grows into a mania; and long after want
has ceased to exercise either pressure or premonition,
unbounded lust of gold rules his heart like a passion,
not to be satisfied even with endless and miserable toil.
The healthy love of sport and battle is transformed into
a tyrannical grinding of the weak, the competition of
business, the villainy of attorneyism and parliamentary
duels, where hired or voluntary gladiators assail one
another with the rapier of speech. Nay even the
salutary and innocent joys of life swell and fester till
even the pursuit of pleasure is a slavery, and that
beautiful goddess becomes the centre of adoring votaries
whose hollow eyes and pale cheeks show how impotent
they are to receive her gifts.

By its intelligence and resolution and ingenuity,
humanity in the mass advances, slowly and steadily it
may be, yet surely. The most hopeful thing we know
of, is that in spite of the declamations of sage and
prophet there is a steady progress in knowledge and
wisdom and goodness. But the advance is not uniform,
Though the race is pressing onward, individuals, classes,
and even entire nations drop out of the running and

allow themselves to drift backward. Many who imagine themselves at the van of progress or the victims of over-civilisation really live the life of mere barbarians. Poor butterflies of fashion hastening from crush to crush, their mouths filled with tittle-tattle and gossip, their brains vexed with problems of dress and equipage; jaded youths who flatter themselves that because they are *blasé*, because they have been 'plungers,' have dipped into forbidden pleasures, visited notable spectacles, and met remarkable men, they have probed the secrets of life; professional and mercantile men who are bound hand and foot to some device for making money, beyond which speculation does not soar; literary persons who for hire play the acrobat or mountebank in news-sheet or magazine, and like the music-hall singer, the shadow-grapher, and the comedian dub themselves artists—those who in the estimation or themselves are the *crème de la crème*—in good sooth what are they but water drops churned into foam, and flung to the wind as a great torrent rushes along its rough and stony course. If we recollect that Carlyle's gaze, as by some horrible fascination, was held to these aspects of modern life, we may well forgive him his loud scorn and loathing of this 'age of shams.'

Wordsworth's way of rebuking these tendencies was like Thoreau's, gentler and not less effective. Out of Babylon he fled away to his home among the hills, and found there a sanctuary where Nature smiled like a kind goddess, and lulled him into forgetfulness of all 'the dreary intercourse of daily life' and

> 'the fierce confederate storm
> Of sorrow barricaded evermore
> Within the walls of cities.'

He and the worldling settled at opposite poles of a sphere. And his value to us is not that of example, but in his serving as antidote to the other's bane. Walden Pond is fair, but not on its shores is the world's work done; pleasant is the gleam of Windermere and majestic the shadows of Helvellyn, but they yield no enduring calm to him who by gazing is not deafened to the battle-cry—

'Forward, forward let us range,
Let the great world spin for ever down the ringing groves of change.'

If Nature is really divine, if through sorrow and death and suffering she is steadily advancing to any definite goal, every impulse and instinct within us proclaims that not by still admiration but by courageous effort shall we best forward her design.

Man always has had an inexplicable faith—more trustworthy perhaps than many a more lucid and reasonable belief—that, though it be by ways dark and inscrutable, all things work together for good. Nature apparently so cruel is still a beneficent mother. Though she light and blow out again a million lives as a candle is set aflame or extinguished in what appears to be wantonness, yet the result is an added glory and richness of life, as if the ultimate aim were to fashion a transcendent intelligence.

But he who conceives this as a bare possibility will no longer refuse to share in the ecstatic enjoyment of the poet. As long as life is itself a gladness death must ever be the mournfullest thing we know of, and no sane and healthy mind will ever quite sympathise with those who hymn it as blessed. It is the one isly phantom whose appearance brings us close to

despair. Nor is any sophistry able to educe from pain
and suffering visible comfort or advantage. A moaning
and wailing from these sound as accompaniment to
all rejoicing. Yet it is needless to magnify their
import. Whether they are the blind accidental griefs
of existence or prudently devised phenomena in a great
design, they are at least inevitable, and it is as useless
as it is natural to mourn them. Indeed a million
distractions fortunately blind the majority in all except
evil hours to their existence. Just as with them life's
play and its actors are everything, its curtain and board
and scenery of minor consequence, so they are so
wrapped up in petty business or pursuit that they
require something to awaken rather than to drug their
sympathy with suffering.

Right as it is for us to know and feel something of
the sadness and melancholy that cast their sober
mantle over so much of the universe, it is no less
desirable to avoid a too morbid gloating over them, and
to feel and appreciate the joy that, in spite of artificial
restraints, is awakened by the happy carol of a bird, the
glow of sunshine, the gambol of younglings, the beauty
of landscape. At times when the conviction steals
upon us that whatever Nature is we are also, till we are
ready with St. Francis to claim brotherhood with sun
and wind, and hail even the last pale visitor as Sister
Death; when we believe with Darwin, as well as the
poet, that every glistening little flower and green herb
has its own ego, its consciousness of pleasure and pain,
then we may turn to Wordsworth as the supreme high
priest of the mystery. Others have fabled to us of
Naiads of the stream and deities of grove and dell, of
Pan singing among the rushes and Priapus lurking in

the garden, but when he speaks to us it seems as though
his very soul had become interfused with the spirits of
wind and earth and running stream so that he is no
longer an individual spectator describing a picture but
a pipe through which universal consciousness is fluting
its song—' He murmurs by the running stream a music
sweeter than its own.'

And it is not for us to quarrel with the note because
it is too pleasant. From the time when David penned
his melancholy Psalms up to now sorrow never has
lacked its singers. Hardly is there one immortal book
the reading of which does not provoke to sadness; the
mirth of Cervantes himself ends in tears, like the
tragical fifth Act of Biography. Where an apparent
gaiety is sustained ofttimes it is but a mantle courage-
ously worn to conceal a cracked and breaking heart, as
dying Hood kept up his punning for bread even in full
view of Death's beckoning finger. Gaiety is so
often strained and unnatural, that it is scarcely cynical
to ask when laughter is loud where the sorrow is
which it is cloaking. But Wordsworth's cheerfulness
is as unforced as a baby's smile, as sincere as its earliest
prattle.

And it is a beautiful fact in regard to life, that as it
were by sympathy alone the spectator shares in every
manifestation of joy. The greybeard, whose sportive
days have long been overpast, still as he watches the
gambols of children feels a spark of his old glee come
back, and he is indeed an exceptional individual who
feels no pleasure in the play of kitten and puppy, of
skipping kid and dancing gamesome lamb, in the
unwieldy caracole of the pasturing cart-horse, or the
sober frolic of kine. Nay we love to fancy that joy

makes the earth look beautiful; that the lily is a living eye out-looking from an inner sea of beauty, and the rose blushes in its own innocent happiness. At such times the poet seems to be but enunciating a commonplace when he says—

> ' —with an eye made quiet by the power
> Of harmony, and the deep power of joy,
> We see into the life of things.'

For a moment the very rocks and mountains seem to smile to us and proclaim the existence of Infinite Being. But again, like fickle gleams of sunshine wandering over a clouded landscape, the light passes away. Gone past recall is the

> ' — presence that disturbs me with the joy
> Of elevated thoughts.'

Around there is only a wilderness of dead matter, and the poet's song has ceased to have more significance than the grating of ice on an empty polar sea, the lament of the wind as it travels over untrodden wastes of snow. What is left of pleasure is only an affinity of matter with matter, the play of light and colour and fragrance upon the senses they have fashioned.

Scepticism is roused whenever Wordsworth endeavours to give any reason for the hope that was in him. It will not credit him when he says—

> ' The being that is in the clouds and air,
> That is in the green leaves among the groves,
> Maintains a deep and reverential care
> For the unoffending creatures whom he loves.'

It refuses to believe that the babe brings with it to earth anything from a previous existence, and it is doubtful even of 'the light that never was.' When he descants on the charms and colour and raiment of earth, or sets forth his worship of Nature, we listen as to a passionate lover's praise of his mistress, as we do to Solomon's bridal song or Dante's sonnets to Beatrice; but we feel by no means sure of his having correctly divined the causes of his passion. No more than do any of the 'creeds outworn' does his belief in the Divinity of Nature drive away all doubt.

What his example actually proves is, that a sane and healthy man, without precisely knowing why, may derive as much joy from earth as any carolling bird or wild creature, and that when this enjoyment is purely sensuous his readers share it without doubt or cavil; when it springs from some transcendent rapture it makes us ask without hope of an answer whether it is based on delusion or on a sure and deep insight into the unsolved mystery of existence.

Printed by T. and A. CONSTABLE, Printers to Her Majesty, at the Edinburgh University Press.